MORE PRAISE FOR THE REAL ATHLETES GUIDE:

RONNIE LOTT, FOX SPORTS, FORMER NFL STAR

"I was happy to contribute to this book because it's packed with vital information about what it takes to succeed in sports, school, and more importantly, life."

RICK TELANDER, ESPN THE MAGAZINE

"Complete, comprehensive, and easy to read. A great benefit to any young athlete considering playing sports in college."

DALE BROWN, FORMER COLLEGE BASKETBALL COACH

"If you're interested in becoming eligible, read the NCAA Guide. If you're interested in getting a meaningful education, read *The Real Athletes Guide.*"

BILL WALTON, NBC SPORTS, FORMER NBA STAR

"This book reveals the inner working of college sports so that athletes can take charge of their lives. Our young people are in trouble. Parents should read this desperately needed book to help their kids."

JANET M. JUSTUS, NCAA DIRECTOR OF EDUCATION OUTREACH

"...excellent insights into recruitment, including rarely stated truths...a must read for prospective student-athletes."

DR. KATHLEEN GABRIEL, ACADEMIC ADVISOR, U. OF ARIZONA

"Athletes must prepare for college success in high school. This book shows them how—in an entertaining, inspiring way."

DARRIN NELSON, ASSISTANT AD, STANFORD UNIVERSITY

"Every potential student-athlete should read *The Real Athletes Guide* prior to picking a college or university. This is one of life's most important decisions; the book helps athletes choose a place and setting where they will be happy and productive and not just consider sports. I will definitely have my sons read this guide when they reach college age."

BOB CORB, PH.D., SPORTS PSYCHOLOGIST

"Finally, a book for student-athletes and their parents that cuts through the hype to address the real issues. Read this book before you make any decisions about college."

JOEL CORRY, SPORTS AGENT

"If an athlete doesn't want to be exploited or taken advantage of, the first step is to read *The Real Athletes Guide.* Then they need to take action."

BOB BENDER, HEAD BASKETBALL COACH, U. OF WASHINGTON

"This book is right on target. It helps athletes make informed decisions about all the critical issues they face from the time they enter high school through their college years and beyond."

JOSEPH HALPER, FORMER COMMISSIONER OF
    RECREATION OF NEW YORK CITY

"The writing and the cartoons express key points in a way that high school and college athletes will enjoy."

KRISTA BLOMQUIST, PRO BEACH VOLLEYBALL PLAYER

"This book is an excellent motivational tool for high school and college athletes who want to succeed. Tells you exactly what you need to know and what actions you need to take."

BILL DONLON, BASKETBALL COACH, LAKE FOREST HIGH SCHOOL

"I've been involved in high school and college basketball as an athlete, coach, and parent. This book sets forth outstanding guidelines for recruiting and preparation for college."

JERRY WAINWRIGHT, HEAD BASKETBALL COACH, UNC-WILMINGTON

"...the most comprehensive guide to recruiting ever written. Must reading for prospective student-athletes and their families, and even coaches."

DAN KREFT, PRO BASKETBALL PLAYER AND WEB DESIGNER

"If this book had been around when I was in high school it would have saved me a lot of grief."

CHRIS MYERS, Fox Sports

"After years of interviewing athletes, I have found that the ones who are the most grounded understand self-accountability. *The Guide* teaches this important lesson."

ERIC ALLEN, NFL PRO BOWL CORNERBACK

"*The Guide* provides a tremendous game plan for high school and college athletes to succeed on the field and in the classroom. You know if Ronnie Lott is involved it's going to be first-rate."

The Real
Athletes
Guide

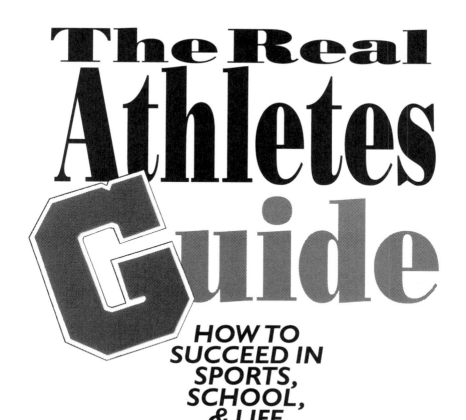

The Real Athletes Guide

HOW TO SUCCEED IN SPORTS, SCHOOL, & LIFE

Marc Isenberg
and **Rick Rhoads**

Athlete Network Press

Publisher's Cataloging-in-Publication

Isenberg, Marc, 1967-

The Real Athletes guide : how to succeed in sports, school and life / Marc Isenberg and Rick Rhoads ; Pregame by Ronnie Lott ; Halftime by Ann Meyers Drysdale ; Postgame by Mike Krzyzewski.

p. cm.

LCCN: 97-095337

ISBN: 0-9666764-0-8

1. College athletes-Handbooks, manuals, etc. 2. College sports-Handbooks, manuals, etc. 3. College athletes-Recruiting-Handbooks, manuals, etc. 4. High school athletes-Recruiting-Handbooks, manuals, etc. 5. Athletes-Recruiting-Handbooks, manuals, etc. I. Rhoads, Rick. II. Title.

GV350.5.I83   796.071

ATTENTION ORGANIZATIONS, ASSOCIATIONS, CONFERENCES, LEAGUES, AND SCHOOLS:

Quantity discounts are available on bulk purchases of this book for educational purposes or fund raising. Special books or book excerpts can also be created to fit specific needs. For more information, please contact Athlete Network Press, PO Box 34867, Los Angeles, CA 90034 or email info@athletenetwork.com.

To my grandfather,
Alfred (Babe) Holtz,
for giving me the confidence
to turn dreams into reality.

— Marc Isenberg

To my Dad,
Professor Lester Rhoads,
a real athlete and a real scholar.

— Rick Rhoads

REALITY CHECK

South Coast doesn't exist

To illustrate key points in the book, we describe events in the lives of several athletes and coaches. The problems are real, but the characters are fictitious. So are Mercury Shoes. We also write about the inner workings of the athletic department at South Coast State University, uncovering tales of deceit and corruption, as well as admirable behavior. This school doesn't exist, any more than does its arch rival, North Coast. A parent who read a draft of *The Guide* asked us for the phone number of the South Coast volleyball coach. After a miserable recruiting experience, the athlete's father thought "Kelly Hughes," whose story begins on page 78, would be the ideal coach and teacher for his daughter. Although we had to explain that we had invented the whole thing, we're pleased that it sounded so real.

We are not the NCAA, the NAIA, the NJCAA, nor any other body that governs your life

We're confident that *The Real Athletes Guide* is the authoritative book on its subject. We've interviewed hundreds of athletes, parents, coaches, academic advisors, compliance officers, and NCAA, NAIA, and NJCAA officials to be sure we're giving you correct information. But, as much as we might like to, we don't govern college sports. The groups with the initials do. The NCAA rule book is ten times as thick as *The Guide* (and 1,000 times less readable). The rules change every year. So if you need to clarify a particular point, please check with the NCAA, the Initial-Eligibility Clearinghouse, or with the many knowledgeable experts dedicated to serving student athletes. If you're dealing with a college governed by the NAIA or NJCAA, check with them. If you screw up, no governing body will accept as a defense, "*The Real Athletes Guide* said I could do it."

ACKNOWLEDGMENTS

In May of 1994, I went to UCLA to research a freelance article on whether student-athletes should be paid. Wayne Johnson, who worked in the UCLA Athletic Department, arranged for me to speak with over 50 student-athletes. I was blown away by the knowledge and insight of this group, which included Ed O'Bannon, Tyus Edney, George Zidek, Toby Bailey, JR Henderson, Lisa Fernandez, Karim Abdul-Jabbar, J.J. Stokes, and Donnie Edwards. After I spoke with them, pay for student-athletes seemed trivial relative to a range of more fundamental issues. The athletes gave me the idea and the motivation to write this book. They started me asking questions and more questions, and talking to more people—athletes, coaches, parents, counselors, administrators, and psychologists. This in turn led to a memorable 4-hour interview with legendary UCLA coach John Wooden. The number of people who contributed to this book began to add up. If you find *The Real Athletes Guide* useful, it's because so many people generously shared their time and wisdom.

Rick Rhoads, as a writing partner, you are great. As a friend, even better. Dan Kreft, you came through in the clutch. More than once! Thank you for your design of the Web site, and for your slam dunk editing. Deirdre Leclercq, you believed in me and the project from the beginning. Special thanks to the Advisory Board of Rick, Dan, Deirdre, Joel Corry, Richard Sherrill, John Carlin, Ann Victor, Bob Corb, and Mike Murray for much-needed guidance and action. Mom and Dad, your love never wavered. Ronnie Lott, Ann Meyers Drysdale, and Coach K, thank you for believing in this project and lending your time and names to this book. Sebastian Conley, it was a pleasure to work with you to put our ideas into cartoons. You got the message—and added to it. Without the proofreading of Katy Leclercq and Peggy Rhoads, our message about attention to detail might have lost credibility. Larry and Renee Anenberg, your support has kept this effort going.

The people at the Amateur Athletic Foundation, including Anita DeFrantz, Mike Salmon, Ed Derse, and Wayne Wilson, provided a meeting place, research, and always looked for others who could help. People who work in the trenches as academic advisors, like Kathleen Gabriel, Jack Rivas, Wayne Johnson, and Fred Stroock never get the credit they deserve for the work they do with student-athletes. Their contribution to this book is invaluable. The NCAA staff, including Steve Mallonee, Bill Saum, and Janet Justus, helped ensure this book's technical accuracy, as did Kevin Henry of the NAIA. The original Real Athletes — Stephanie Wasserman, Krista Blomquist, Lisa Griffith, Chris Johnson, Anya Kolbisen, Antawn Jamison, and Murriel Page — shared their experiences on our Web site and helped bring this book to life.

Other people whose involvement has been invaluable:

Leigh Steinberg, Bill Walton, Rick Telander, Dale Brown, Holly McPeak, Bob Costas, Riza Manning, Margoleath Berman, Jeff Fellenzer, Chris Myers, Bob Ibach, Keenan McCardell, Margaret Akerstrom, Stuart Glassman, Eric Allen, Bob Bender, Shantay Legans, Tom Hoffarth, Marty Anenberg, Mike Holtrey, Barry Temkin, Darrin Nelson, Marques Johnson, John Carlin, Sue Levine, Nick Zaccagnino, Bill Bennett, Jackie Hamlett, Andy Bark, Brentt Eads, Rob Miech, Jerry Wainwright, Mike Wimmer, Steve Appel, Milt and Avis Henderson, John Bailey, Rick Majerus, David Eyl, George Raveling, Ralph Jackson, Jim Harrick, Steve Krone, Brian Snerson, Bill and Mary Ann Donlon, Brian James, Bob and Doris Leclercq, Arnie Wexler, Shirley Ito, Risa Gordon, Lester Rhoads, Howie Garfinkel, Quin Snyder, Carlos Gomez, Joe Paterno, Eric Joss, Jim Sysko, Mike Shay, Al Hergott, Peter Rudman, Adam Rudman, Brentt Eads, Kenn Miller, Becky Heidesch, and many more.

If people find this book easy on the eyes and easy to use, it's because we had the best in business working with us:

Cover Design: Linda Tobin

Page Layout: Pacific Publications

Indexing: Katrina Lemke

—*Marc Isenberg*

CONTENTS

LIST OF CARTOONS

PREGAME

by Ronnie Lott

Let me tell you a story to show why *The Real Athletes Guide* can make a big difference in your life.

During my freshman year at Southern Cal, I was put into a game for one play with instructions to do nothing but cover the tight end. Instead, I tried to sack the quarterback. I wanted to be the hero. I was within inches of the quarterback when he completed a 1-yard touchdown pass to the wide-open tight end. The extra point put our arch rival UCLA up 27-26 with two minutes to play. Fortunately we kicked a last second field goal to win the game.

I had ignored my assignment, acting as if I knew more than an experienced coach. It was a devastating mistake, but I was determined not to let one play ruin my career. Every day that summer I went to my high school practice field. I lined up in front of an imaginary tight end, and "covered" him in every defense USC used. It had to look crazy to anyone watching, but I was determined to prove that I could be counted on.

What can you learn from this story?

- You are responsible for your success. If you want something, do all the things, large and small, necessary to attain it. I'm talking about success as an athlete, and, even more importantly, as a student and all-around person.

- Everyone makes mistakes. Don't be afraid to make mistakes, and don't make excuses. Face up to your mistakes and learn from them, or you cannot succeed.

- Don't get burned by your ego. I had been taught to sacrifice my individual wishes for the good of the team. But against UCLA I tried to be a star instead of focusing on what the team needed from me.

Never underestimate how far these ideas can take you. The San Francisco 49ers won four Super Bowls in the 80s. Many so-called experts said that Joe Montana wasn't big enough for a quarterback and didn't have a strong enough arm. They said Jerry Rice couldn't make the transition from Mississippi Valley State football to the pros. They said I was too small to be an NFL safety. Other teams had athletes who were bigger, stronger, and faster.

What does it take to succeed?

Everybody in the 49er organization knew his role and took personal responsibility for helping the team win. Ownership and management were the best in the League. They made sure we had all the tools necessary to win, from a state-of-the-art training facility to charter flights to away games. They provided the resources for the coaches and general manager to get the best talent. Head Coach Bill Walsh took a total business approach to winning, from long-range strategy to the smallest detail. Our players looked for every advantage—conditioning, off-season training, nutrition, mind exercises. Anything to gain the upper hand. If you convinced some 49ers that their play would improve if they wore lipstick, the next day at practice you'd see a lot of guys sporting shiny red lips. To be a 49er you had to be committed to doing all the large and small things necessary to achieve excellence.

When people made mistakes our attitude was neither to blame nor excuse. We used the mistake to learn how to do it right.

If your attitude was, "Look at me, I'm a great football player," you did not fit into the 49ers. On the field we blocked out distractions such as money issues and the media. We respected ourselves and each other because we focused on the basics that got us to the top: hard work and perseverance.

Another team might have been bigger, stronger, or faster—on paper. We didn't care. Life is not about how you measure up on paper, whether it's your 40-yard time or your SAT score. It's about wanting something bad enough to do what it takes to get it. My teammates knew I would go to war for them in every game.

Dumb jock myth

To be a success, you have to get an education. Most athletes are not going to make their living from their sport after college. That's just reality. Statistically, you have a better chance of becoming a brain surgeon than a professional athlete.

When I arrived at USC, I promised myself that I would get my degree. I did not buy into the "dumb jock" myth. You have to be disciplined, competitive, and smart to excel as an athlete. These are the same qualities needed to succeed in the classroom. Why go to college and not graduate? It seems stupid, but too often athletes look at college only as a step to the pros. It's okay to dream that you will make the big time. But if you are mature, you realize that your dream might not pan out. I remember being so tired after practice that I had to force myself into the library, force myself to open a book, and force myself to concentrate. I knew that if I tried to just get by in the classroom, sooner or later it would catch up with me.

To be a success you have to get help from others. I was fortunate to have parents, coaches, and teachers who supported my goals and dreams, who gave me guidance and instilled discipline. I purposely surrounded myself with friends who were motivated to succeed and who supported each other.

Who do I want to become?

Every day, on TV or in the newspapers, you hear about college or professional athletes who have committed crimes, become addicted to drugs or alcohol, abused women, or become involved with illegal gambling. Why do these athletes risk their careers, freedom, and health? It's not because they are happy and secure. Something is out of balance in their lives. Despite their success in sports, these athletes are not satisfied. They become their own worst enemies.

When you know who you are, and where you want to go, it's easier to decide what to do. But sometimes we are so busy practicing our sport or meeting other time-consuming demands that we forget to take stock of our values. When that happens, we risk making decisions that hurt our chances to get what we really want out of life. All of us need to step back once in a while and ask ourselves, "Who am I, and who do I want to become?" As a young person, these questions are especially important for you, because most of your life is still in the future.

Use *The Guide* to focus on the universal characteristics that will make you a success in whatever you do.

Former NFL defensive star Ronnie Lott won four Super Bowls with the San Francisco 49ers. He is now a commentator for Fox Sports.

THE REAL ATHLETES CREDO

Real Athletes

► Treat their sport with respect.

► Don't look for the absolute minimum, on or off the field.

► Work on fundamentals without coaches' orders, and study even when no assignment is due the next day.

► Understand that sports is not forever and that education will help secure their futures.

► Don't cheat in school even if they know they won't get caught.

► Know that it's team play that wins.

► Give back to the community, even when the media is not there.

► Set goals and plan to reach them.

► Measure success not by wins and losses, but in knowing they've put forth their best effort.

► Know that failure is part of the road to success.

► Play to win, but *not* at all costs.

► Promise only what they can deliver.

► Set examples for others to follow, not because they want to be role models, but because that's who they are.

► Know right from wrong.

Part One

OVERVIEW

SHARK PROTECTION FOR ATHLETES

CHAPTER 1

WELCOME TO REAL ATHLETES

It's fun to be an athlete. And it brings special opportunities to get an education, meet people, gain recognition, and develop skills you can apply to every area of life.

Sounds too good to be true? Right. There is a downside. Along with the special opportunities come special dangers. The big business of high school and college athletics does not label the opportunities and dangers. In fact, they often come packaged with the same glitter. "Stay eligible. Take this easy course. Your tutor will even 'help you' (wink) write the paper." Is that a break? Or a trap?

The athletic establishment is like the ocean. It's big and filled with sharks. *The Guide* reveals the shark hangouts, so that you can jump in and enjoy the water without worrying about what lurks below. None of us can succeed without help, and there is no better way to get help than from studying the good and bad moves others made in trying to

- balance athletics and academics
- cope with the special treatment and mixed messages given to some athletes
- make friends and find mentors
- select the right college and handle the pressures of recruitment
- prepare for a career
- develop a system of values

Entertain and amuse

Our goal is to entertain and amuse as well as empower you. After all, we say that you can work hard for success and have fun at the same time. If we bore you to death, we'll lose our credibility.

To put it another way, we are not Ph.Ds (nothing against folks with advanced degrees) and we have not written a (pardon the expression) textbook.

How to benefit from *The Guide*

We urge you to read the entire book now, to get the big picture. Then, as you go through school, go back over parts of *The Guide* to help you deal with opportunities and obstacles as they arise.

By getting the big picture, you won't end up in situations like these:

- It's your senior year in high school, and you're dreaming about continuing your sport in college. Suddenly you get a wake-up call! You take the SAT for the first time, and you score 680. There's little chance for you to reach the required score within a few months. *The Guide* shows you exactly how to prepare and when to start.

- You're a college freshman, and you just found out that your coach is leaving. You were a top student in high school and excelled as an athlete—you could have been accepted at just about any college. You selected this school primarily because of the coach. Suddenly, you realize you don't like the place. It's too cold, too big, too far from home, and the department in your major sucks. *The Guide* shows you step-by-step how to select a college based on all the factors that are important to you.

The earlier in your life you read *The Guide*, the better. But the information is useful whether you are a high school or college athlete, whether you are a "blue chip" recruit or an average player, whether you play basketball or football or compete in a non-revenue-producing sport. And whether you are male or female.

We encourage you to share this book with key adults in your life. There is even a special message for parents or others you look to for advice, in Appendix A.

If you are already in college, the portions of the book most relevant to you are Part Two, "Success;" Chapter 9, "College Athletics 101;" and Part Four, "The College Years."

If you are still in high school, the whole book will help you succeed.

There is a special briefing for pro prospects in Chapter 15, "Jumping to the Pros."

Chapter 2, "Greater Opportunity for Women," will interest male as well as female readers.

Everybody will want to read the Pregame by Ronnie Lott; Halftime by Ann Meyers Drysdale; and the Postgame by Mike Krzyzewski.

Why AthleteNetwork.com?

We started out to write a book. As we interviewed hundreds of athletes, parents, coaches, teachers, and athletic advisors and administrators, we were swept away by the breadth and depth of their knowledge, and their eagerness to share it. And by their ability to describe their experiences and beliefs with drama, eloquence, and humor. It dawned on us that we wanted to create a live network that you could plug into, enjoy, learn from, and contribute to, 24 hours a day, 365 days a year. A nationwide community of athletes. The Internet, a revolution in communications that enables people to share knowledge in ways unimagined just a few years ago, made that possible. So we started a Web site, AthleteNetwork.com.

The Guide helps you to see high school and college athletics as a whole, and to focus on questions that affect many athletes. AthleteNetwork.com allows you to talk directly to other athletes about your exact situation, and to offer your experiences and views to help them with theirs. You can also draw on the experience of parents of athletes, former athletes, coaches, and athletic advisors.

You can make friends online, and of course the Web site deals with issues as they happen, while any book, once it is published, is frozen in time.

Visit AthleteNetwork.com to learn, share, challenge, chat, and laugh. You have nothing to lose. It's free.

Been there:
A personal word from Marc

Experience qualifies me to speak on the problem of balancing athletics and academics. Sad experience. I was forced off the Emory University basketball team because I did not take academics seriously. By NCAA standards I was eligible, but the coach saw that I was not living up to my potential in the classroom. In fact, often I wasn't in the classroom. I still regret that my college basketball career ended this way, but I'm grateful to Coach Winston for his wake-up call. I earned a degree in finance at Emory, but my real education was in playing, reading, and following sports. Many of my study sessions in the library were spent reading their back issues of *Sports Illustrated*. My real major was the business of college athletics. (I was learning more about finance than I knew.) Looking back, at age 30, I've hopefully learned from my mistakes. And, while I didn't get college credit for what I spent most of my time doing, all is not lost. Much of what I did helped prepare me to write this book. (Really, Dad!)

When I decided to write this book, I thought "Piece of cake, six months and we'll be published." That was four years and 31 publisher and agent rejections ago.

Why did I press on? Because even if the so-called experts believe there isn't enough of a market to succeed financially, I still think there is a need for this book. If I'm wrong, oh well. Athletics gives you a wonderful opportunity, but it can also be the source of great disappointment and confusion.

I teamed up with Rick Rhoads, who is not only a great wordsmith, but also added an older (and much wiser) perspective. Our goal of writing this book is to provide you with useful information, in your own language, which can help you thrive in sports and school.

Most of all, we believe what we say in *The Guide*. Anything in life that's worthwhile takes hard work and perseverance. There are no magic formulas for success. No shortcuts. You are the judge of the outcome. I can tell you that writing this book has been a great journey. *—Marc Isenberg*

It's a great life if you don't weaken: A note from Rick

Marc is about the same age as two of my three daughters, so I bring a different perspective to these pages. I've participated as a parent in the college and graduate school selection process, and even been called on for advice in career decisions. Raising kids— and being raised by them—has been a rough but rewarding voyage. Especially rough during their teenage years. My wife, Peggy, and an eye on the big picture, helped me survive.

So did laughter. Stuff can be serious and funny. During the hundreds of hours Marc and I spent together writing this book, we laughed so loudly that my wife would ask, "Are you working?" We laughed mostly about things that happen in sports. About crazy things and even about horrible things, like the father of a football player who sharpened the buckle on his son's helmet to cut opponents. Laughing beat crying.

I was a swimmer in high school. Once in college, words became my game. (After all these years, I wish they came easier.) But I still remember my best time in the 100-yard freestyle. In fact, it gets faster as I get older. From swimming, and later from running 10K races, I learned to compete with myself, to always try to improve. Of course, things are more complicated when you can't measure them on a clock. We've edited and rewritten this book many times, in an effort to make it as clear and useful to you as possible. Let us know what you think of *The Guide*, and what you get out of it, and you'll help improve the next edition for the athletes who come after you. Thanks. *—Rick Rhoads*

CHAPTER 2

GREATER OPPORTUNITY FOR WOMEN

Teenage movies in the 1950s often featured the football captain and the head cheerleader. Today, thousands of female athletes know what it's like to hear the crowd roar for them. "Power and speed and in the lead" is replacing "sugar and spice and everything nice."

Why is it so important for girls to play sports? It's simple. Girls should be athletes for the same reasons society places such emphasis on boys being athletes.

We hear a lot about the alleged differences between males and females. Little boys are aggressive, so sports is the perfect outlet for them. Little girls are docile and fragile, so they should play at being wives and mothers.

What a bunch of #$@$%! Have the perpetuators of this myth ever seen a girls' soccer game?

Male or female, there is no better training ground for life than participating in sports. Buzzwords that are synonymous with success in corporate America originate in the sports world: teamwork, leadership, goal setting, determination. Recently, we've seen the explosive growth of "executive coaching." Playing with dolls just does not compare to sports as preparation for success in life.

M or F, athletes are athletes

Of the many choices kids make growing up, there is no better or more important decision than to participate in sports. Thankfully we live in an era where it's cool for females to play sports.

We can quote all the statistics which prove that girls who participate in athletics have higher self-esteem, are more likely to stay in school, and less likely to get pregnant or use alcohol or drugs. And you know that those women soaring over hurdles or running a fast break on the basketball court are not the ones trying to prove their maturity by sucking on cigarettes.

Ultimately, it comes down to the fact that sports is more fun—and far more exciting and rewarding—than hanging out at the mall.

Title IX, a federal law, mandates gender equity in sports. Many people are under the impression that Title IX passed just recently. Actually it became law in 1972. Unfortunately, the NCAA and its member colleges didn't comply for a couple of decades. It took a bang on the head from the US Supreme Court. Now, finally, the sports world is wide open for females. Of the 248 teams added by NCAA schools in 1996-97, 227 are women's. To achieve gender equity, many colleges are actively recruiting women for athletic scholarships.

Title IX didn't happen by itself. Hundreds of women who excelled at athletics and fought against the barriers in their way proved that the stereotypes were false. Among the most notable are Babe Didrickson, Billie Jean King, Peggy Fleming, Wilma Rudolf, Lyn St. James, Bonnie Blair, Chris Evert, Jackie Joyner-Kersee, and Martina Navratilova. Ann Meyers Drysdale, who wrote the "Halftime" for this book, is the only woman ever to have a tryout for an NBA team.

The 1996 Olympics in Atlanta showcased women's athletics as never before and served as a springboard for greater exposure and opportunity. Women's professional basketball has re-established itself in the United States. The process of involving women in sports on an equal basis with men isn't complete, or we wouldn't have had to write this chapter.

It's a great time
to be a female athlete

Participating in sports is fun and rewarding immediately and in the long run. It prepares you for career success and more. It can start a lifelong habit of working out, which is a must for long-term health and well being. It's not automatic, as is obvious from the bad shape some athletes find themselves in when their competitive days are over. But it's a great head start. It's important to get into the habit of being active—working out, running, playing sports.

Boys raised as athletes; girls as proper young women. That's the way it used to be. It will never be the same again. *Vive la différence!*

Part Two
SUCCESS

CHAPTER 3

INGREDIENTS FOR SUCCESS

The Guide outlines everything you need to do to succeed in high school, to select the right college for you, and to succeed at college. Doing well in college will give you a running start toward achieving success for the rest of your life—the years, hopefully 60, 70, or 80 of them, after your college graduation.

There's a lot that goes into success. In high school, you've got to balance sports, academics, social life, responsibilities at home, and maybe a part-time job. You need to take the right courses and prepare for college entrance exams. You've got to select the right college, which can be complicated, particularly when the pressures of recruiting come into play. Once at college, the demands of athletics and academics both become greater, but you still have to balance them. You've got to select the right major and begin planning to go on to graduate school or start a career. Even social life gets more serious as you find lifelong friends and perhaps even a spouse.

Doing all of this well sounds hard, but life is in many ways a juggling act. If you're not feeling pressure, check your pulse. Just pay attention to the details, understand how each detail helps achieve your goals, and you can succeed and enjoy the process. When you work at it, it's not as hard as it looks at first. One accomplishment leads to the next accomplishment. After a while, success becomes habit forming. It can't be all that hard: lots of people have succeeded who are not any smarter than you. It's doable and enjoyable, particularly when you make good friends along the way.

But there are many ways to fail in our society. Plenty of people find them. You can spot classmates who are on their way. If you read *The Guide* from a different angle, it provides detailed directions on how to fail. Just do everything the book says not to do, and we guarantee you will fail or your money back.

If you'd rather succeed, what are the key ingredients?

Passion

When you were a little kid and you went on a trip with your family, did you drive your parents crazy by asking, "Are we there yet?"

What's wrong with that question? It makes the destination the reward. Successful people agree that the journey is the reward. They love what they are doing, even when they are struggling to reach their goal. The harder the road, the sweeter it is when you get to your destination.

For lasting success, find something you are passionate about, including the tough parts. Something you enjoy doing, thinking about, and talking about. A goal that captures your imagination. A journey that, like a good story, you don't want to end.

Balance

Passion leads to success, but unlimited passion can mess you up. That's where balance comes in. Let's say you play basketball. If you practice shooting, but ignore dribbling, passing, and moving without the ball, you probably won't feel good about your chances of success. Or, let's say you work hard to make $10 million, but you mistreat everybody around you so that you end up rich but surrounded by enemies. Would this be success?

Balance means paying attention to all the important things in your life. It also means keeping an eye on the future as well as the present. You might say, "I'm happy when I play ball, run, or swim, but I'm not happy when I read books (except this one) or sit in a classroom." Do you think the same things will make you happy in five, ten, or twenty years? If not, shouldn't you do what you enjoy now, while also working hard at things that seem difficult or boring, but that are necessary for your future happiness? If you don't do these things during your high school and college years, there will be consequences down the road. When you tackle challenging tasks, especially those you think you're not capable of, you may surprise yourself with your abilities—and with how satisfied you feel.

Perspective

As great as sports is, we shouldn't lose sight of the fact that in the grand scheme of things it's really pretty small. If you're a young athlete living in an ESPN world, it may be difficult to comprehend this. However, ask someone who has experienced the death of a family member or has been stricken by cancer how important the state finals are. It's fine to get caught up in the excitement of sports, but it's also important to be able to put it all into perspective. What are your priorities in life? Do you live for the moment, not worried about what lies ahead? Or do you realize that when you're done playing competitive sports, there are decades of life to live?

Consistent hard work

"The harder I work, the luckier I get" is a common expression. Those with the discipline to work hard consistently over a long period of time are ready to take advantage of a break when it comes along. Your smarts, talent, personality, and good looks will take you a certain distance. But as you grow up, you enter the competitive world. Without putting in the necessary effort, you don't stand a chance against those who develop the habit of hard work. We've all seen cases where an athlete had so much talent that he or she excelled without trying. Suddenly, the others catch up, and the athlete gets frustrated at no longer being the star. The same thing happens to some students who find it easy to get good grades. They never develop the study habits necessary for success in the long run.

Work often gets a bad rap in our society. Try an experiment. Ask people of any age what they like to do. We predict that most will reply with something from this list: "Go to the beach, go skiing, listen to music, play ball, go shopping, hang out, watch TV, travel, dance, see a movie." A few will say they like to read. Hardly any will say they like to work or study.

Why not enjoy doing the work necessary to turn your dreams into reality? Isn't that more satisfying then lying on the beach? The joy of the beach fades when you know you've been ignoring your responsibilities. The beach is enjoyable as a break from hard work. It's the icing on the cake, not the cake itself.

Preparation

As an athlete, you know the value of preparation. Preparation begins with a plan. To succeed you've got to practice a lot, but you also have to practice smart. You have to know which skills to work on now, which later. You have to know what kind of strength training and conditioning your sport requires. To do well you need to visualize where you want to be—a week, a month, a year, several years from now. Then you need to make an overall plan about how to get there, and break it down into steps you can achieve each day. When you're a kid, adults do most of this planning for you. As you get older, more of the responsibility is on you.

Preparation is equally necessary for success in other areas of life. For example, suppose a college you're interested in requires that you take advanced algebra. You would need to know that early in your high school years, so that you could take the courses that lead up to advanced algebra. Finding this out in your senior year would be like learning just before the start of a game that you were supposed to study the playbook. Or like showing up for a swimming meet without your bathing suit.

Coach John Wooden, who led UCLA to 10 NCAA men's basketball championships in 12 years, said "Failing to prepare is preparing to fail."

Maturity

As we grow and learn more, we should see how big the world is, how infinite the knowledge, and just how little of it each of us really grasps. Therefore, we should become more open to advice, suggestions, and help from others. Of course, as we gain experience, we should evaluate all advice critically, even when it comes from people we trust and hold in high esteem. There's a joke that college freshmen think they know everything about a subject after reading one book about it. Then they read another book, which contradicts the first book, and suddenly they know much less than they thought. But it's no joke that know-it-alls rarely succeed. Even those that do well for a while get left behind when life moves on and they are unable to grasp new developments. Anyway, a big part of success is having friends, and nobody likes a know-it-all.

Initiative

If it's your job to take out the garbage, and you do it when you're told, that's obedience. If you see the garbage container is full and you take it out, that's initiative. Initiative is closely related to maturity. Nobody expects a 2-year-old to be a self-starter, except in tearing up the place. As you get older, success requires doing what the situation requires, and not waiting for your parents, teachers, and coaches to spell out every detail. Initiative even requires finding out what is required. Say you miss a class because of a road trip. Do you find out what took place in that class, including any assignments, or do you just wait for the ax to fall?

Seeing the big picture

Life is under no obligation to give us what we want. Sometimes we have to do things not because we want to, but because they are steppingstones to what we really want. You might choose a school where you won't play as much as a freshman, but that will serve you better in the long run. You might take a job with less pay, but which offers better training and experience.

Whatever you decide you want to become, long-term success requires attention to things that don't necessarily provide immediate payoffs. When you focus only on your sport you miss the big picture. By remaining ignorant of the world around you, you set yourself up for a fall. It's happened to many professional athletes who were once rich and famous, then just famous. Their money disappeared. It reappeared in the hands of others.

Ignorance allows you to be taken advantage of. By educating yourself you earn the respect of others. It's similar to what happens when you're part of a team. You want respect from your teammates, so you work hard to prepare for your role.

What really motivates us? It's not only money. Sometimes money is just the way we keep score. We want other people to accept us, to value our ideas and opinions. Above all to respect us.

When your athletic career is over you want to be ready to go on to other successes. It's fine to pursue a dream. But putting all your hopes on making it big in professional sports is like staking your future on winning the lottery. It would be great, but it's not likely. No matter how talented you are, you're never more than an injury away from the end of your athletic career. Your plan should prepare you for success no matter how far you go as an athlete.

Values

Get to practice. Get ready for a math midterm. Write an English paper. Get to your part-time job. Watch your little brother. We have to run fast just to stay in the same place, let alone to advance.

What happens to the things that are most important to us? Our relations to family and friends? Our ethical or religious beliefs? Our concerns about society? When we are constantly rushing around it's easy to lose track of our basic values…and it's tempting to take shortcuts.

Maybe you take money from an agent without thinking through the consequences. Or you accept a good grade without doing the work. Or drugs are going around at a party, everyone seems to be enjoying it, and you join in.

A shortcut will always get you somewhere…but it's rarely where you want to go. All of us need to step back every so often and ask ourselves, "What's it all about? What kind of a person do I want to be? What should I be thinking about when I make decisions?" When you are young and changing fast, these are critical questions. One way or the other, you will become an adult.

You can pay attention to how you grow and develop—or just let it happen any old way. Why not direct your own production?

These big questions are tough to deal with. In Appendix B we have broken them down into parts to make them easier to handle. Only one of the parts is about sports. You might think the other parts are unimportant. If we say that athletics should not be the number-1 priority in your life at this time, you might reply, "Are you kidding?" But throughout your life, your priorities will change. Picture yourself ten years from now, perhaps with a spouse and children. You don't want to regret that you neglected to prepare to be productive outside sports.

And, finally, a sense of humor

If you never crack a smile, you can depress yourself and those around you.

Even grim situations have their funny side. In one of Jack Benny's classic jokes, a robber confronts the comedian (who cultivated a reputation for being cheap) at gunpoint and demands, "Your money or your life!" After several seconds of silence, the robber says, "Well??!!!" Benny replies, "I'm thinking, I'm thinking."

If someone disrespects you, is it best to brood about it, fight about it, or laugh it off? Sure, it depends on the situation, but laughter is often the best way to put the incident in its proper perspective.

People with well developed senses of humor can laugh at themselves. In the "Pregame," Ronnie Lott talks about learning from mistakes. That's really the main way we learn anything, whether it's our sport or how to act our age. By definition, when we are young we are "guilty" of a lot of immature behavior. Changing and learning new skills is often difficult. It can be frustrating, depressing, and, sometimes worst of all, embarrassing. If you can pick yourself out of the mud and laugh about it, rather than wallow in your misfortune, it can help you recover and advance. And people will like you for it.

So, take life seriously. And lighten up!

CHAPTER 4

TAKE RESPONSIBILITY FOR YOUR SUCCESS

We all need a lot of help. But ultimately success is up to each of us.

We live in an imperfect world where some people have more opportunity than others. Discrimination persists despite the many advances that have been made in the struggle for civil and human rights. There is no question that it is hard to succeed when you're worried about getting enough to eat, or when you have to get past drug pushers on the way to school.

But if you just blame things you can't control, you can't win. It's useful to identify the obstacles to success, *if you then figure out how to overcome them.* If you don't take that second step, you are justifying failure. That may make you feel better for the moment, but it won't solve your problems. It's like saying, "I just can't run fast," instead of, "If I do wind sprints, I'll learn to run faster."

You can inherit money, but you have to work for success

Success requires being ready to take advantage of opportunity. You've got to be prepared to prove you can do the job. Some so-called experts say there are groups that cannot succeed because they are genetically inferior. What is their excuse for supporting such unscientific ignorance? Who are they to discourage some young people from becoming whatever they want to be? No one is handed success on a silver platter. You can inherit money. You can even inherit being seven feet tall. But you have to work for success.

Former athletes often blame lack of success on the system of college athletics: "They used me to make money for their athletic program, but they didn't try to teach me. When they had gotten everything they could out of me, they threw me back where I came from."

That could be half true. Athletic success for a college or even a high school means winning. Some athletic directors, coaches, and teachers are not concerned about the welfare of their athletes and don't try to help them succeed. Even those who are concerned make mistakes.

But it's also half false. To remain eligible and uneducated, an athlete has to cooperate in deception. The athlete may believe he or she is beating the system, but in fact the athlete is losing out on an education. The bottom line: If you want to get educated, you will.

How to succeed after you don't

Success almost never comes as the result of a straight path to the top. Typically, there are ups and downs. Everybody knows the story of Michael Jordan being cut from his high school basketball team. Instead of becoming discouraged, Michael worked harder to improve. He became even more determined to get what he wanted. Develop the inner confidence not to give in to disappointments, but to overcome them. You can do that by looking beyond a momentary setback and figuring out what you need to do to recover and advance.

How to fail fast

You cannot succeed by destroying yourself. Unfortunately, today's reality offers a number of ways of doing just that, including drugs, booze, tobacco, crime, sleeping around, and road rage.

Sometimes people harm themselves or take foolish risks because they feel overwhelmed. It can be hard to talk to friends and family about what troubles you, but try to do it. Your problems will usually look less overwhelming and easier to deal with. If necessary, talk to a professional counselor.

Steroids, creatine and andro

Many athletes have used steroids to become stronger and faster. The problem is steroids make you crazy and destroy your health, sometimes leading to death. Every organization that governs sports, from the International Olympic Committee to the NCAA, bans athletes who test positive for steroids. For all these reasons, don't take them.

In the 1990s a muscle-building supplement called creatine has become popular with athletes. Some doctors think creatine may harm the kidneys and other organs, or cause emotional changes. So far, studies are inconclusive. No one knows the long-term effects, just as no one in the 1950s knew the long-term effects of smoking cigarettes.

A professional athlete who happens to be really strong and breaks home run records takes androstenedione (andro), a substance legal (as we write) in Major League Baseball, but banned by the NCAA, NFL, and IOC. Does this mean you should run out to your local GNC store and start using andro?

There's nothing wrong with looking for whatever advantage you can. As long as it's legal, and much more important, is proven not to be harmful. That's the problem.

The label on Andro-6 contains this caution: "Because of the potency of this formula, Andro-6 should not be used by women, anyone under 18 years of age, or people suffering from any medical conditions, including, but not limited to, diabetes, heart disease, psychological disorders and prostate hypertrophy."

Creatine and andro are available over the counter. As "nutritional supplements," they are not regulated by the Food and Drug Administration. Unlike pharmaceutical products, there are no requirements for animal and human research studies before

© 1999 AthleteNetwork.com

they are made available to the public. Because they are not classified as foods, they are not even subject to food labeling laws. So bottom line, you don't really know what's in the bottle. One athlete failed a drug test after taking a product labeled "Chinese Herbal Medicine." It contained steroids.

Before you start taking supplements, ask yourself if you're doing everything you can to improve your strength and quickness. There are no shortcuts to success in sports. Usually, the answer isn't a pill or powder, but a lot of hard work.

No doubt other magic potions are on their way to the locker room. We urge you to avoid unproved and potentially dangerous substances, even if they are not banned. Don't risk your life for a marginal advantage.

Athletes and crime

These days it's hard to tell the sports pages from the police blotter. There are hundreds of talk show hosts, journalists, and psychologists who tell us why so many athletes break rules and commit crimes. It really doesn't matter why. All that matters is that you figure out right from wrong, and know how to stay out of trouble.

It's really not that hard. There's a famous saying: "The best defense against the bomb is not to be there when it goes off." It's the same with avoiding trouble. Don't get yourself in situations where trouble is even a remote possibility. And if you find yourself where trouble is about to happen, get yourself out of that situation...quickly!

As an athlete, certain aspects of your privacy are invaded. It's the good with the bad. If you hang out in places or with people where trouble always seems to follow, like with gangs or in bars, you have to accept the fact that these groups of people are not making the best decisions in the world. There are plenty of examples of athletes who are confronted by drunks but who walk away. Those are the stories you don't read about in the paper. Hanging out in bars can be inviting trouble. It goes with the territory. Then the next day on TV the athlete claims that his actions were warranted because he felt a threat to his life.

Sometimes the best thing to do is suck it up and not retaliate. One athlete said, "I had no choice but to retaliate, because he tested my manhood." Grow up. You need to keep your cool even if the person deserves to be punched in mouth. It's just not worth risking your career. You might be convicted of assault. Think jail time. And you don't know who you are dealing with. The guy can pull a gun and shoot you. As they say, cemeteries are full of people who made bad split-second decisions.

Friends you can count on

It's a dog-eat-dog world. Who can you trust?

But how can anybody be successful without a few close friends? You share your thoughts, goals, and fears with friends. Friends help you understand the world, and understand yourself.

To a large degree, your success or failure is determined by whom you surround yourself with. The wrong friends drag you down. "Peer pressure" is on all those lists of reasons why people get drunk or take drugs. The right kinds of friends lift you up, like a point guard who raises everybody's level of play. Of course, there will be times when even the right friends make bad decisions. That's when your independent judgment and self-confidence will see you through.

You're going to spend a lot of time in high school and college with your teammates, and some of them will naturally become close friends. You might have to go out of your way to make a close friend who doesn't participate in organized sports. It's worth the effort. You need a friend who has a different viewpoint.

Part Three
THE HIGH SCHOOL YEARS

CHAPTER 5

ENJOY HIGH SCHOOL...AND SUCCEED

High school sets the tone for the rest of your life. If that doesn't sound encouraging, there's still time to change direction. Step one—read this chapter.

How can you enjoy being a kid while becoming an adult? How can you cope with the additional responsibilities in your life? Your challenge is to have fun and grow up at the same time.

Enjoy your sport and your life

It's easy to get depressed or angry when things don't go your way. In your sport, you may think the referees made some horrible calls, even cost your team the game. But, when your truly analyze the situation, was it the bad calls that cost you the game? Or would better execution throughout have won it? In sports, bad calls have a tendency to even out. The same goes for life. You may not always get what you want, but if you keep working hard, eventually you'll catch some breaks. The key is to not to get bent out of shape when things don't go your way. Have a positive attitude in whatever you're doing.

Just think about what you are doing

How to handle pressure

There's pressure to win in sports. The pressure may come from your coach, your teammates, your fellow students, your parents, or yourself. If you like to compete, you'll probably respond well to the pressure. Athletes with a strong desire to win understand that practicing hard and playing hard are absolute necessities. Even if it's difficult or boring at times, they see the value of hard work in the big picture.

The best results come when you respond to your own pressure to excel, and block outside pressures. Think of a good foul shooter with the game on the line. Opposing fans may be screaming and waving streamers. The shooter hears nothing, and sees only the rim. Winning in athletics and in life means focusing on the task at hand.

How to deal with problems

Satisfaction in athletics carries over to other aspects of your life, and vice versa. You can't really separate them. So if you find yourself troubled by something in athletics or otherwise, ask yourself why. We all have a tendency to put off problems, hoping they will go away, but deep down we know they won't. So don't let a problem get you down without trying to do something about it. There may not be an immediate or total solution. But you'll feel good knowing that you've identified the problem and that you're taking a step toward solving it.

Learn or get burned

You are surrounded by teachers (Don't panic!) who spent four years in college, and maybe went to graduate school, read umpteen books, did countless hours of research—all to prepare themselves to give you information and insight.

You could say, "No thanks, I'm not interested." Or you could grab all the knowledge you can.

Maybe you don't believe science, math, literature, history, and geography, or the ability to speak foreign languages are all that necessary.

Think about the value of knowledge in your sport. Could you be a basketball player without knowing what a pick-and-roll is? Does a baseball player have to know about the squeeze play? A football player about the draw play? A swimmer about stroke mechanics? A runner about pace?

Knowledge plays the same role in the game of life. Without knowledge, you are lost. History, for example, tells you where you are. History tells you what has come before that has shaped you and your community. It gives you clues about the future.

There's no future in blaming the teacher

You might think that some of your teachers are not good at teaching. You might be right. Certainly not all teachers are equally committed to their profession. There are great teachers and good teachers. Others are burnt out: they've become discouraged and stopped trying. Still others have a knack for making fascinating material boring beyond belief.

Students who are not doing well in a course often blame the teacher. Even if the teacher is bad, that's a mistake. If you don't learn, the teacher doesn't pay the price. You do. So ultimately you are responsible for figuring out how to learn the material, whatever it takes.

Homework: the mystery revealed

Teachers assign homework because (select only one)

a) They want to make your life miserable.

b) Reading 30 book reports makes their weekend.

c) They don't realize South Park is on TV tonight.

d) It's required punishment for original sin.

e) None of the above.

"Do your homework" has come into our language as a phrase that means "Be prepared," whether you are talking sports, business, or school. Similarly, "She does her homework" is a description of a person ready to succeed in any area. Clearly, the phrase originates in school. Is it possible that teachers pile on homework to help you learn? Does that mean we should think it's important and do it, even if it means postponing surfing waves, channels, or the Internet? Does copying a classmate's math homework count as "doing your homework"? We will not insult your intelligence by supplying the answers.

Beyond homework

Novelist Walker Percy said, "You can get all A's and still flunk life." Those of you who get poor grades may be nodding your heads and saying, "Yeah. I'd rather be street smart than book smart." You might even resent "nerds" and "bookworms" who ruin the curve.

The reality is most A-students are doing just fine. Those with street smarts and good grades do better in life.

Let's go one step further. There is a huge body of knowledge beyond street smarts or homework. Most of it can be found in books, magazines, and newspapers. If you make reading a habit, you'll learn and be entertained at the same time.

One problem with reading is that it cuts into music, TV and videogame time. We all need diversions. But how many hours a week do you spend watching TV and playing video games? What do you get out of it? Will it help you achieve your goals, or would you be better off reading? This brings us to a newly discovered schism in our society.

What Persuasion are you?

Many people say our society is divided by race, gender, or wealth. There's some truth to that. But did you ever stop to think that the main division in our society is between People of Smart Persuasion and People of Dumb Persuasion?

We're born with no predisposition as to which category we belong to. As we grow and mature we gravitate toward one Persuasion or the other. It's up to you to determine whether you fall into the Smart Persuasion or whether you'd look right at home on *Jerry Springer*.

What does it take to get with the Smart Persuasion?

More than anything else, what you are doing right now. Read. It's that simple. Sorry if this sounds like an infomercial for reading.

If you don't read, you learn only from your own experience. But in a lifetime of reading, you learn from thousands of others as well. You can draw upon world-class experts in every field: sports, politics, business, philosophy, religion. Reading about things that interest you helps you define your goals and develop a plan to accomplish them. You can read books about Michael Jordan, Tiger Woods, Lisa Leslie, Colin Powell, Kevin Costner, Oprah Winfrey, Denzel Washington, even George Washington.

Once you start a well-written book, watching a typical TV show reminds you of a visit to the dentist.

Does reading depend on race, gender, or money? No. Reading is for everybody.

Reading is one activity where it doesn't hurt to get comfortable. Lie back on your favorite couch, let the remote control fall from your hand, and pick up a book.

Reading does not suck

In fact, it's fun. Sometimes reading gets a bad name from books that are forced on us. People associate reading with being told, "You must study pages 34 to 67 in our dusty old history textbook by tomorrow." Even the vastly talented People of Smart Persuasion have a hard time reading material that's flat boring.

Nobody likes being told what to read, even if it's a great book. The teacher says read the first chapter of Moby Dick, and you're already thinking Cliffs Notes. It shouldn't have to be that way. Many books are exciting, especially when you're reading them because you want to.

As an athlete, you've got to love a magazine like *Sports Illustrated*. It's one of the best written publications in the world.

© 1999 AthleteNetwork.com

Check out your local newspaper or a national newspaper like *USA Today*. You'll find articles and opinion pieces that interest, provoke, and even outrage you. Look beyond the sports section, or you'll miss fascinating stuff that opens your mind and ensures your place among People of Smart Persuasion.

Reading is habit forming

When you're out of shape, it's hard to drag your lazy butt into the gym. But when you're in the habit of exercising—and you see the benefits—it's hard not to work out. It's the same with reading. Once you get in the habit, you're hooked. You can't stop. You might want to act dumb, but it's hard. You've absorbed so much knowledge. And you can't help thinking about what you read. You talk about it with other people. Next thing you know, you're hanging with people who read, who think, who have ideas. You've joined People of Smart Persuasion.

How to get good grades and fail

Let's say you are flunking a course, but you are the high school phenom. There may be pressure on your teacher or an administrator to change your grade, or to find someone to do your work for you. Some teachers won't go along with this; others allow themselves to be pressured into it; some get caught up in the excitement and lose sight of their responsibilities.

The question is, Do you help yourself by accepting this kind of "aid"? Keeping you eligible this way may help a coach's career. It may result in more wins, so that the community is happy. But what does it do for you? It makes you eligible...but dumb. It teaches you to look for the easy way out, a habit which is guaranteed to lead you into trouble. This kind of "aid" is far worse for you than money and gifts from people with their own agendas. Those can cost you your athletic eligibility, but faking grades can cost you your ability to think.

Be open with your parents

Your parents (we won't keep adding "or other advisors") have your best interests at heart. That's why they told you not to eat candy before dinner. Or to do your homework before you watch TV. If they didn't care about you, they wouldn't bother.

Nevertheless, many young people ignore their parents' advice. Big mistake. Your parents have lived a lot longer than you, and they want to give you the benefit of their experience. You may not take all of their advice, but you can only gain by listening to it and considering it.

Do you think your parents are too inflexible in their efforts to get you to do what's right? That's possible, but try to be open to your parents' advice, and to be open with your parents about your thoughts and feelings. You can learn from each other. Just keep in mind who's got the edge in experience. When you're 45 years old, who do you think will have a greater understanding of life? You or your teenage children?

The path to success crosses a college campus

What's the connection between college and success in life?

- If you want to continue competing in your sport after high school, college is the place to be. It's where you can get the coaching, the competition, and the support from fellow athletes necessary to reach your potential.

- By continuing in your sport, you can further develop habits such as hard work, discipline, cooperation, and confidence that will help you in whatever you do.

- College is where you are trained to deal with information. In the Information Age, most good jobs require a college degree. For many, flipping burgers is the only alternative to a college education.

- At college, the greatest opportunity to learn is outside the classroom. You can meet people of varied backgrounds, from all over the country and the world. You can discover a wide range of knowledge that will benefit you for the rest of your life.

CHAPTER 6

PREPARE FOR COLLEGE

If you enjoy learning, preparing for college will be relatively easy. You won't have to be concerned about meeting the minimum standards for college entrance, because you'll be far above them. Most colleges will be open to you.

No one comes along and says, "Listen, just be stupid, don't learn anything, don't prepare for college." Instead, they throw curve balls. They invite you to a party. You say, "I've got a test tomorrow, I've got to study." They put pressure on you: "This party's gonna be cool." They don't even have to add the rest of their message, that studying is uncool. You think that you don't want to be a nerd. You want to be one of the guys. This is just one test and there will be plenty more. Sometimes the curve ball has a little extra spin on it: "Let's get high," or, "Let's get drunk." As usual, how you respond comes back to who you are and who you want to be.

Opportunities in college athletics

Wherever you go to college, the purpose is to get the best education possible, experience new things, and become prepared to succeed in the real world. If you plan to play sports in college, there is a wide variety of rewarding opportunities, from big-time college basketball on national TV to lacrosse played in front of friends and family standing at the sidelines. From team sports such as volleyball and hockey to individual sports such as wrestling and track and field.

To take advantage of the opportunities, you need to know about the National Collegiate Athletic Association (NCAA). The NCAA is the largest of the organizations that govern college sports, with over 330,000 athletes at 1,200 member schools. Its rules on athletic scholarships and eligibility to participate in athletics are also the most complex, with different requirements for each of the NCAA's three divisions. Even if you don't end up attending an NCAA school, you'll probably consider them as part of your decision-making process. Or you might end up transferring into an NCAA program. So we'll take you through the NCAA requirements and then cover the other options.

What is an athletic scholarship?

NCAA Division I and II colleges are permitted to award athletic scholarships: financial aid to athletes who meet the organization's eligibility requirements, regardless of their financial need. The grant is awarded one year at a time, and "may be renewed each year for a maximum of five years within a six-year period." Division III colleges do not have athletic scholarships. According to the NCAA, their scholarships must be based only on financial need and academic achievement, and cannot be based on athletic ability. Of course, if you qualify, you can receive financial aid up to the full cost of attendance from any college, independent of your participation in athletics.

Full rides

What most people call an athletic scholarship or a "full ride," the NCAA refers to as a "grant-in-aid." The nice thing about this "grant" is it's not a loan. Once you get it, you don't pay it back. Certainly the ideal scenario is to get a full athletic scholarship. This basically covers everything—tuition, room and board, books, and, if your school or coach has a sweet deal with a shoe company, free shoes and apparel. With all the talk about paying college athletes, full scholarship athletes have it pretty good. The opportunity to get a free education is an enormous advantage. Just ask a recent college graduate who is faced with a mountain of debt.

Partial scholarships

The NCAA limits the number of athletic scholarships a college can offer in each sport. However, not all schools can fund the maximum number. For instance, men's baseball is allowed 11.7 scholarships. Budget constraints might limit a school to six. Instead of offering full scholarships to six athletes, the coach might spread the money out by offering partial scholarships to, say, 12 athletes. Chris Cardinal wants to play baseball at the collegiate level. Two Division I baseball powers have offered him scholarships. South Coast State University offered Chris a 1/5 scholarship, while Cadwallader College offered him a 1/2 scholarships. If Chris must choose solely for financial reasons, which school should he pick? Hint: It's a loaded question. Cadwallader, a private school, charges tuition of $25,000. Tuition at South Coast is $8,000. Hopefully you paid attention to algebra because you're going to need it now. Brian's financial obligation would be $6,400 at South Coast and $12,500 at Cadwallader. In this case, 1/5 is better than 1/2. But, not so fast. Schools can help you combine a partial athletic scholarship with Pell Grants and other non-athletic financial aid.

Other roads to college

You can go to college even if you don't get an athletic scholarship. If you need financial aid, there are aid packages available from the government and from colleges that depend on your family's financial need, not on your athletic ability. These packages include outright grants, work-study (aid in return for doing a part-time job at the college), and loans.

You need to work hard at finding what's available. There are billions (yes, billions) of dollars out there for people who want to attend college. Because a lot of other deserving students are looking for loans and grants, it's important to start early. Many programs require you to fill out forms which ask for a ton of financial information. They also have strict deadlines (read: don't be a day late sending in your application). Get your parents involved; they may belong to unions, churches or other organizations that offer scholarships. Visit your school's college counselor. Get on the Internet. Go to the library. Don't wait for your athletic scholarship to come through. You don't want to be left without the option of attending college because you didn't plan ahead. Is this book beginning to sound like a broken record? Be thankful. You are getting this information at the expense of others who made these mistakes.

If you have the will to get an education, you will never be shut out from attending college. No matter how poor a background you come from, college is always an option. You may have to join the Armed Services for a couple of years, work full- or part-time, fight, scratch, and claw. It would be easier to have a full ride, but won't this be more fun? Maybe not. But you'll appreciate it more.

Walking on

You can continue your sport in college even if you did not get an athletic scholarship. A coach who thinks you can contribute to the team will be happy to have you participate as a "walk-on." Actually, most walk-ons are recruited. A coach may not have a scholarship to offer or may not want to commit one. So he encourages you to attend his school, telling you that you are likely to get an athletic scholarship by your sophomore year. This can work out well. But go into it knowing that if you do not perform up to the coach's expectations, you won't get the scholarship.

Athletic scholarships are awarded one year at a time

Don't be fooled—there is no such thing as a guaranteed 4-year full ride. NCAA regulations prohibit a college from promising to automatically renew an athletic scholarship. An award cannot be taken away during the school year based on poor athletic performance. A coach can, however, choose not to renew a scholarship. An athlete must be notified of non-renewal in writing by July 1—a disastrous time to try to get into another college or arrange for other financial aid. If you feel your scholarship may be in jeopardy, ask the coach about your future immediately (but not right after you drop a pass). By NCAA rule, an athlete can appeal non-renewal to a committee outside the athletic department. There are no NCAA guidelines for these committees, so they vary from school to school. Committees tend to support athletes if they feel non-renewal is related only to performance or injury. But they generally support coaches who can show that the athlete violated a team rule or the school's conduct code.

So what happens if an athlete is injured, doesn't make an effort, or fails to live up to expectations for some other reason? Some athletic departments and coaches are more concerned than others about their obligations to athletes. But all coaches are under pressure to win with a limited number of scholarships. Scholarships taken up by unproductive players don't produce victories.

At South Coast, the football coach helps players who are not contributing transfer to colleges that can use their abilities. But last year he had a sticky situation: a player who was happy at the school and did not want to transfer. The coach started looking for reasons not to renew that player's athletic scholarship that would be acceptable to the appeal committee. For example, an academic problem or a violation of college regulations. There have been instances at South Coast where football stars have had their scholarships renewed when they've hardly been to a class or when they were under indictment for a crime. But for an athlete who is not helping the team, flunking one course or breaking a minor dormitory rule might be used as the basis for not renewing a scholarship.

Renewing partial athletic scholarships

Partial scholarships can be abused because they have the potential to be increased. Say you're offered a 1/4 scholarship, and the coach holds out the possibility of a full ride after a couple of other players graduate. This is a slippery slope. Scholarships are not supposed to be pay-for-play, but if you don't perform on the athletic field, the coach might not increase the scholarship.

How to safeguard
your athletic scholarship

The NCAA denies that having an athletic scholarship is similar to being an employee of the school. But the bottom line is that you are under pressure to perform to earn the financial aid, just as an employee must perform to earn a salary. An athletic scholarship ties you to a team. You'd like to concentrate on your sport, and enjoy it, without the pressure and distraction of knowing that your ability to stay in college is tied to your performance.

How can you safeguard your athletic scholarship? Here are our suggestions:

While being recruited

- Try to select a program in which the level of competition is realistic for you. If you are a high school superstar, and big enough and strong enough (in sports where that matters), that could be a top Division I team. If you are not a superstar, think twice before joining a program where you are likely to be one of the most expendable athletes.

- Ask recruiters if the program will recommend that your financial aid be renewed each year even if you are injured. The NCAA does not permit recruiters to say that financial aid is automatically renewed. But they are permitted to say that they will always request renewal, and that the financial aid department has always followed their recommendations in the past.

- Ask a coach's current and former players what happens to recruits who don't measure up to expectations. Does the coach renew their scholarships or look for reasons not to renew? Does the coach help them transfer or make their lives miserable so that they will quit and free up a scholarship?

In college

- Do your schoolwork and follow the college rules. This is the game plan for success. If you depart from this game plan, you will fall behind and have to play catch-up.

- Protect yourself from illness and injury by taking conditioning seriously and maintaining healthy eating and sleeping habits.

Earning an athletic scholarship

Let's say you've decided to go to college, and you think that earning an athletic scholarship is the best way for you to get there. You might believe that to get an athletic scholarship you should concentrate on your sport, and do just enough to meet the NCAA minimum requirements for college admission.

We hope you reject that strategy because getting the grades you want does not mean getting the knowledge you need. But aside from that, this strategy is only half right. You do need to work hard to improve your athletic skills, rather than rely on raw talent. But you also need to do well in school. Almost every coach says that grades are a critical factor in selecting athletes for scholarships. Coaches refer to athletes who are achieving only the minimum as "academically marginal." They know that these students are most likely to flunk out of college or be unable to maintain eligibility. Coaches are afraid to risk scholarships on academically marginal athletes. And they wonder if an athlete who won't study the math book will study the playbook.

Preparing for college: the details

Once you've decided to prepare for college, how do you do it?

Get the free NCAA Guide

The National Collegiate Athletic Association (NCAA) rules most of the kingdom of college sports. It determines the eligibility of athletes to practice and play in college, and the rules that govern the awarding of athletic scholarships. For example, an NCAA rule allows a Division I women's college basketball team to award 15 athletic scholarships. Each year the Association publishes the latest version of its *NCAA Guide for the College-Bound Student-Athlete*. The rules in effect during your senior year will determine your college eligibility. But there are lots of things in the pamphlet that you need to know when you are in ninth grade, such as the high school courses required for eligibility.

The pamphlet may be available from your high school. If not, you can get it free from the NCAA. Call the NCAA Hotline toll free at (800) 638-3731 and request the *NCAA Guide for the College-Bound Student-Athlete*. You can also use this system to get recorded answers to questions and to order the *NCAA Guide for the 2-Year Student-Athlete*. NCAA information and publications are also available online at www.ncaa.org. Or send a request to

NCAA
6201 College Blvd.
Overland Park, KS 66211-2422

This address should be good until August, 1999, when the NCAA plans to move its headquarters to Indianapolis.

Know the rules...or else

You may think that some of the NCAA's rules are unfair or absurd. But like it or not, they are the rules you must live by if you want to participate in NCAA-sanctioned sports. If you don't learn the rules, you could inadvertently break them and place yourself in jeopardy of losing your eligibility or your scholarship.

Talk to the right people at your high school

It's your responsibility to alert your counselor of your intention to play college sports. That way, the counselor can help make sure you take the right courses and prepare properly for college entrance exams. An advisor might be an expert on college requirements, but might not know the intricacies of the NCAA rules. To participate in athletics during freshman year, an athlete has to satisfy the requirements of a particular college, and also the requirements of the NCAA. We cannot stress enough the importance of understanding exactly what is required of you. Find the relevant parts of the NCAA pamphlet, show them to your advisor, and ask questions to make sure you are doing everything necessary to satisfy the NCAA.

Guidance counselors are not the only people who can advise you. Your coach may be able to help. Or talk to a teacher you respect. The teacher will usually be pleased to help.

Don't settle for college counseling that doesn't start until junior or senior year. To be sure you're doing everything necessary to be eligible in college, start thinking about these issues in ninth grade.

Don't rely totally on one advisor

Compare what one person tells you with what another tells you. Evaluate everything you are told. Even excellent counseling cannot substitute for thinking for yourself. Spend a lot of time considering all your options, and avoid hasty decisions. It's your future, and you are in charge of making it come out right.

Take the right courses

If you don't take enough "core courses" in high school, you will not be eligible to compete in college. You'll find information about core courses in the *NCAA Guide for the College-Bound Student-Athlete* and from your high school guidance counselor. Core courses must be academic courses, such as English and math, but not every academic course is automatically a core course. Non-academic courses, such as drivers ed., phys ed., sex ed., metal shop, and cooking are not core courses. Remedial courses, even if they are in academic areas, are not core courses.

For all the details about core courses, including how many years of each subject you need, read the *NCAA Guide*. These are the subjects, according to the 1998-99 *NCAA Guide*, on which core courses must be based: "English, Math, Social Science (history, social science, economics, geography, psychology, sociology, government, political science, or anthropology), Natural or Physical Science (biology, chemistry, physics, environmental science, physical science or earth science), Additional Academic Courses (foreign language, computer science, philosophy, or nondoctrinal religion)."

To be eligible to participate in athletics at a Division I or Division II college, you have to successfully complete at least 13 core courses. Your grade point average in those 13 courses must be no lower than 2.0 (a "C" average). But it pays to do better (aside from learning more). As your grade point average moves up, your minimum required college-entrance exam score for Division I eligibility goes down. The NCAA publication has the details. Once you get your grade point average to 2.5 (a "C+" average), you've reached the maximum benefit in lowering the minimum SAT or ACT scores. Of course, you increase your chances of being admitted to the college and athletic program of your choice by having an average in the 3.0–4.0 range (a "B" to an "A" average).

Don't limit yourself to the minimum number of core courses. Studies have shown that academic success in college has little relationship to SAT or ACT scores, but is closely related to doing well in lots of core courses. Aim for taking 16 to 20 of them.

The road to eligibility passes through the Clearinghouse

The NCAA has created the "Initial-Eligibility Clearinghouse." Behind this catchy title lurks something important to you. To be eligible to participate in Division I or Division II athletics as a college freshman, you must register with the Clearinghouse. The Clearinghouse must certify that you have satisfied grade point average and core courses requirements.

Until recently, the Clearinghouse determined which courses in your high school qualified as core curriculum courses. Now it is the responsibility of your high school principal to make that determination. What will the NCAA do if it comes out that a high school principal is signing off on bogus core courses? As we write, no one knows; the situation hasn't come up…yet.

Your high school must submit certified core courses to the

Clearinghouse on Form 48-H. If your school does not often send athletes into Division I and II programs, it may not have filed Form 48-H. If you intend to play in Division I or II, it's (Surprise!) up to you to make sure they have. You can get a free copy of the Initial-Eligibility Clearinghouse brochure and form by calling the NCAA Hotline at (800) 638-3731.

The Clearinghouse hasn't always been adept at handling its responsibility. In one unfortunate case, an athlete who had satisfied the SAT requirement—and had a 3.5 GPA—packed her bags to leave for freshman orientation. But there was a hitch. The Clearinghouse had not made the final determination. When they finally got around to reviewing this athlete's transcript, they determined that an English course did not qualify. This left the unfortunate athlete with 12.5 core courses, 0.5 below the required 13. A legal mess ensued. Yadda yadda yadda. The athlete wasted a year battling through this nightmare. Although she finally won the case, it was a hollow victory because the court did not rule until well into the school year.

Let this be a lesson. First, make sure you know what courses will be accepted as core courses. The time to find out is not when you submit your application to the Clearinghouse. You should know from the time you enter high school. Taking and passing 13 core courses is not difficult if you plan accordingly. Again, don't forget this is a minimum standard. And we hate minimums! You're going to be better prepared for college level work if you've taken 16 to 20 core courses. We feel bad for the girl whose eligibility was overturned, but it could have been avoided if she had done more than the absolute minimum.

Partial qualifier purgatory

Division I and II athletes who come close to meeting the grade point and the SAT or ACT scores may be eligible to practice but not compete during their freshman year. See the *NCAA Guide for the College-Bound Student-Athlete* for details. We hope you won't have to. Invest your time in getting good grades and scores. That is far easier and more useful than trying to grasp the intricate requirements for "Partial Qualifier" status.

Initial eligibility step by step

Start by getting the Clearinghouse pamphlet, *Making Sure You are Eligible to Participate in College Sports*. Ask your college counselors for the Initial Eligibility registration materials from the Clearinghouse. Counselors can call (319) 337-1492 to request materials.

Normally, you register with the Clearinghouse after your final junior year grades are posted on your transcript. High school counselors can waive the $18 Clearinghouse fee if you have received a waiver of the SAT or ACT fee.

) make sure the Clearinghouse has certify you. These include

signed student release form :arly in your senior year)

ɒt, mailed directly from every :tended

ɔres

le to Participate in College Sports here are many. For foreign students, there is a special application, with other requirements.

Aim for good grades

In the first class of the semester, a teacher asked her students, "What grade do you want?" Just about everyone answered, "A." Then she asked, "What grade do you plan to get?" There was a big silence. Most students wanted an "A," but were not planning to earn it. Finally, a few students said "A," some said "B," some said "C." You can bet that very few students who planned to get a "C" ended up with an "A."

You should be out for knowledge, not grades. But there is a relationship between the two. Both require work. You can't just want good grades. You have to plan to get them.

Like practicing for your sport, studying has to be routine. Study at a regular time and place, and avoid distractions.

How to Become a Person of Dumb Persuasion

© 1999 AthleteNetwork.com

Background music is OK, but you cannot study while talking to a friend on the phone. Many students pretend they are studying while actually watching TV. If you believe TV helps you learn, why not take it a step further? Suggest to your coach that your favorite programs be projected on a giant screen during practice.

Perhaps you're having a problem in a class, and you hope that it will go away if you ignore it. It won't. You will just fall further behind. Ask your teacher for help. If a quick explanation won't solve the problem, the teacher might recommend a tutor.

Success does not necessarily mean getting an "A." You may have a terrible time with a particular subject, or you may be digging yourself out of an academic hole. If you honestly give it your best effort, and you earn a "C," that's success. Savvy coaches and business leaders responsible for selecting personnel seek people who are improving. They know that someone working hard often overtakes someone who's doing well, but running on cruise control. In fact, students who do well without a lot of effort, in sports or academics, sometimes believe they can get by without hard work. Later on, when the competition gets tougher, they find out they're wrong.

SAT and ACT

When selecting students, colleges are increasingly giving more weight to high school records and less to test scores on standardized tests. The NCAA, however, requires that you take the SAT or the ACT tests to be eligible to participate in NCAA-sanctioned sports in Divisions I and II.

The *NCAA Guide for the College-Bound Student-Athlete* has information about the minimum SAT and ACT scores required for college athletic eligibility. One interesting NCAA rule: You can combine your highest score on each part of the test, even if they were earned on different test dates. High schools make announcements about when and where the tests are given, or you can check their Internet sites: www.collegeboard.org for SAT; www.act.org for ACT. You can register to take the tests online.

You can take the SAT or ACT more than once. It's a good

idea to take the test for the first time during your junior year. That way, you become familiar with it and you have plenty of time to improve if necessary. Sometimes students put off taking the test because they can't afford the fee. Fee waivers may be available for students from families with low incomes. Ask your counselor.

How can you improve your SAT or ACT scores? Your high school may have a program to help you prepare for the tests. Bookstores sell study guides, and there are commercial test-preparation courses which typically cost several hundred dollars.

Steady learning is the best way to prepare for the SAT or ACT, and it doesn't cost a penny. Work consistently on your core courses, particularly English, for the verbal portion of the test, and Math. Vocabulary and reading comprehension are big parts of the verbal portion, so by reading (even the sports section) you prepare yourself to do well on the college admissions tests.

Coping with learning disabilities

If you suspect that you have a learning disability, such as dyslexia, or another condition which affects learning, such as Attention Deficit Disorder (ADD), it's important to be assessed by a qualified psychologist or learning specialist. Your school is legally required to provide accommodations for learning-disabled students to help level the playing field in doing course work. The SAT and ACT also provide accommodations, such as waiving time limits.

If you're receiving accommodations for a learning disability, contact the NCAA to be sure that your grades and scores will be accepted for purposes of athletic eligibility. The NCAA is skeptical about athletes who fail to meet minimum eligibility requirements and then suddenly discover they have a learning disability. So if you are an athlete who may have a genuine learning disability, it's doubly important to be assessed early.

The NCAA is not the only game in town

Chicago Bulls guard Scottie Pippen played basketball at the University of Central Arkansas for four years before becoming a top pick in the NBA draft. "So," you ask, "what?" Central Arkansas was not a member of the NCAA. It was part of the National Association of Intercollegiate Athletics (NAIA). Currently 349 four-year colleges and universities throughout the United States and Canada belong to the NAIA. More than 57,000 male and female student-athletes compete each year in the NAIA for 23 national championships in 13 sports.

Even though the media make it seem that the NCAA has a monopoly on college sports, that's just not the case. In addition to the NAIA schools, 45,000 athletes at 530 two-year colleges compete in intercollegiate athletic programs under the auspices of the National Junior College Athletic Association (NJCAA). And there are other national associations, such as the National Christian College Athletic Association (NCCAA) and the National Small College Athletic Association (NSCAA). Your choices for getting a college education while continuing your sport extend well beyond the NCAA.

NAIA eligibility requirements

If you're considering attending an NAIA school, read their publication, *Guide for the College-Bound Student*. It includes information on eligibility regulations, financial assistance policies, and recruitment policies. Get their *Guide for Students Transferring from Two-Year Institutions* if it applies to you. Both publications are available on the NAIA Web site, www.naia.org. Or you can request the pamphlets by calling (918) 494-8828 or writing to

NAIA
6120 S. Yale Avenue
Suite 1450
Tulsa, OK 74136

The NAIA is not burdened by billion-dollar TV deals. Depending on what you're looking for, this is a loss or a blessing. One result is that the NAIA does not have the income to support a huge bureaucracy, resulting in less red tape for athletes, high schools, and colleges. For example, there is no Initial-Eligibility Clearinghouse or its equivalent.

In some ways it is easier to be eligible to play your sport at an NAIA college. Entering freshmen must meet two of the following three requirements:

1) A minimum of 18 on the ACT or 860 on the SAT. Tests must be taken on a national testing date. Scores must be achieved on a single test date. This differs from the NCAA requirement, which permits combining a verbal score from one date with a math score from another.

2) A minimum overall high school grade point average of 2.0 on a 4.0 scale. Unlike the NCAA rules, there is no sliding scale that allows eligibility with a lower ACT or SAT score for athletes with higher grade point averages.

3) Graduate in the top half of your high school graduating class.

Achieving requirements 2 and 3 allows you to be eligible without having to satisfy a minimum ACT or SAT score.

2-year colleges and the NJCAA

Accredited junior colleges or community colleges, also known as 2-year colleges, offer Associate Degrees in a number of subjects, and also prepare students to transfer to 4-year colleges. In some cases, athletic scholarships are available. Community colleges benefit students who cannot meet the admissions requirements or financial demands of a 4-year college. Or let's say you want to play Division I sports and you could get into a 4-year college, but you're not yet good enough athletically. You might go to a 2-year college to further develop your athletic skills, especially if you started your sport late in your high school career.

Information from the NJCAA, which governs junior college sports, is available at their Web site, www.njcaa.org. You can request their pamphlet, *Information for a Prospective NJCAA Student-Athlete* online or by writing to

NJCAA
PO Box 7305
Colorado Springs, CO 80933–7305

Entering a community college is easy. Often the only requirement is to graduate from high school, or just to reach age 18. Students who earn an Associate Degree can transfer to a 4-year college if they meet its academic requirements. Athletes who have qualified through the Initial-Eligibility Clearinghouse based on their high school records can transfer and play after one year.

The NCAA annually publishes a pamphlet entitled *NCAA Transfer Guide* to help athletes who want to transfer from 2-year colleges to 4-year colleges. You can order the *Transfer Guide* by calling (800) 638-3731. Warning: you may find mastering differential calculus easier than following the text and charts in the *Transfer Guide*.

When you start high school, why not set your sights on getting into a good 4-year college? If you make that your goal, you are more likely to do the work necessary to achieve it. If you encounter problems along the way, you can fall back on the community college option, which will give you a second chance for admission to a 4-year college.

National Christian College Athletic Association (NCCAA)

The NCCAA provides another opportunity to play sports at the college level. It has a membership of 110 colleges and universities with over 12,000 student-athletes. The organization's mission is to "provide intercollegiate athletics with a Christian perspective." Their eligibility requirements are the same as the NAIA's. You can get information from the NCCAA by phone at (765) 674-8401, on their Web site, www.bright.net/~nccaa, or by writing to

NCCAA
PO Box 1312
Marion, IN 46952

National Small College Athletic Association (NSCAA)

The NSCAA governs sports at 100 colleges, each with an enrollment of under 1,000 students. Information from NSCAA is on their Web site, www.users.lr.net/~dmagee/ or by mail from

NSCAA
113 East Bow Street
Franklin, NH 03235

Getting information on colleges

There are books that summarize information about all the colleges in the United States. They list where the college is, the type of campus (city, suburban, or rural), the number of students, the majors offered, tuition and other costs, the athletic programs, the extracurricular activities, the types of students who attend, the admission requirements, and other information.

These books may be available in your high school library or in the guidance or college counseling office. Or you can find them in public libraries. Things change, so be sure to use a recent edition.

Collegiate Directories publishes a complete listing of collegiate sports programs, coaches, addresses, and phone numbers, *The National Directory of College Athletics*. There are editions for male and female programs. These are great resources for athletes who want to contact coaches. You can order by calling (800) 426-2232 or by visiting their Web site at www.collegiatedirectories.com.

It's never too soon to start thinking about where you want to go to college. Visualize yourself attending the college of your choice—walking around on campus, going to classes, competing in your sport. It can motivate you to work to get there.

CHAPTER 7

MANAGE YOUR TIME

When you read the section on success in high school, you might have thought, "There's an awful lot of things I have to do to succeed!" In college and afterward it only gets more complicated. The cartoon athlete at the front of the book is in a perpetual struggle to balance the academics and sports at the ends of his barbell. A common, more complex image is that life is like a juggling act, with one ball representing career, another family, another social, religious, or political obligations, another leisure and recreation, and so on. How do you keep track of all the balls?

No one is a natural

Being organized—which involves keeping your goals in mind, staying on top of things, anticipating demands on your time, and planning accordingly—is one of the most important skills you can learn. We say "learn" because no one is born with this ability. Think back to when you were a little kid, and your parents pleaded with you to pick up your toys. You probably cried, not realizing the benefit you'd get next time you wanted to play. If you've already mastered organization, great. If you're like most of the rest of us, learning to be organized will be either very hard or extremely difficult. But once you get in the habit of doing things the right way, you'll never want to return to Disorganization Hell. As someone smart put it, "If you don't have time to do it right the first time, when will you have the time?"

"LEAVE ME ALONE!"

Planning for a lifetime

"Lifetime" is an interesting word, the way it combines "life" + "time." It reminds us that we're not here forever. There may be an infinite number of things to do in life, but there are a finite number of hours, days, weeks, months, and years in which to do them.

That doesn't mean we have to compulsively schedule every second, or that we can't have any fun. What would be the point?

It does mean that to accomplish our goals (ours, not somebody else's) we have to plan our time. Each of us remembers more than one weekend when we had to write a paper or cram for a test instead of playing sports or going to a movie with friends. Why? Because we hadn't planned to get schoolwork done. In fact, we wasted a lot of time watching TV, which was nowhere near as much fun as the activities we had to miss. Even quality goofing off requires planning.

Keep it simple

Whole books have been written about time management. This may be overkill. Basically, figure out what your priorities are and make sure you're putting the bulk of your time into those areas. Of course, sometimes you have to handle a non-priority area because it's urgent, like your brother is locked out of the car and you have to bring him the spare set of keys. But think about the last few weeks. Are you always reacting to events, or are you in control? If you spend most of your time "putting out fires" rather than accomplishing your objectives, try to figure out what you can do to change the situation. It will probably help to talk about the problem with your parents, a coach, a teacher, or a friend.

Start with a date book...

Do you know what you will be doing next Tuesday at 4PM? Or four weekends from now? The first step in taking control of your time is to get a date book, if you don't already have one. Date books come in many styles and prices, including electronic organizers. Get one that works for you and fits your budget. If you tend to lose things, do not invest big bucks in an electronic organizer. If you use a computer on a daily basis, consider one of the organizer programs that allows you to print out date book pages. Among paper date books, there are products such as Day Runner® and Day-Timer®, as well as other yearbooks of various sizes and styles. Look them over in a business supplies store such as Staples or Office Depot and pick one that seems best for you. (Banks, stores and other businesses sometimes give out date books as free promotions.)

Some people think they don't need a date book, because they are under the illusion that they can remember all their tasks and appointments. Well, if you hardly ever do anything, that could be true. But then you have a more basic problem. Like, get a life. Among those who have a life, we know one guy — one! — who actually succeeds in keeping all his appointments in his head. He even remembers hundreds of phone numbers without writing them down. But for the rest of us, the odds against functioning well without a date book are worse than the odds of becoming a professional athlete. And, as you recall, the odds of becoming a brain surgeon are better than the odds of becoming a professional athlete.

...and use your date book

Now comes the big challenge. Owning a date book does not organize your life, any more than owning a textbook prepares you for a final. You've got to open it. Frequently. Keep your date book with you, even in your gym bag, and use it on a daily basis. Record homework assignments, practices, games, work, social appointments. Everything. You will be amazed at how easy it is to schedule two activities at the same time if you don't check your date book. Once you've filled the pages with things to do, look in the book every evening or every morning — whatever works for you — to be sure that you are carrying out your plans.

Once a week spend 10 or 15 minutes with your date book. Review how you've been spending your time, and look forward to see if your plans are designed to accomplish your goals. If you're not satisfied, figure out what you need to do and when to do it, and enter that information into your date book.

Scrap the scraps

You don't have your date book with you. You write down an appointment, including the address and phone number, on a napkin. You stick the napkin in your pocket, purse, or book bag. Good luck. If all goes well, you remember the appointment and you don't have a conflict. The worst case scenario: you forget all about the napkin and miss the appointment. Next to worst: you remember but you don't remember where the critical information is. You spend an hour tearing the house apart, then find the napkin in the first place you looked. You have made yourself and your family crazy, possibly uttered a few bad words, and now feel relieved, but foolish. Keep your date book with you and use it.

Use a notebook too

You have a notebook or a section of a notebook for each course you take in school. How do you record other important information? Examples:

- You ask your coach to recommend summer workouts that will help you improve your skills. Coach responds with a series of detailed suggestions.

- Your team is organizing a car wash to raise funds. You are responsible for making the announcements. You've got to write down the date, time, place, price, and other details.

- You're on the phone with a friend who gives you seven possible places to look for a part-time job.

- You go to a presentation on preparing for the SAT. You need to remember dates, places, and the names of some books.

- You earn money baby-sitting. You want a record of all the information parents have given you about emergencies, health, food, TV, bed times, and other details that will help you do the best possible job and make the most money.

- You attend a seminar about selecting a college. You need to keep track of important requirements and deadlines for applications, the Initial-Eligibility Clearinghouse, campus visits, and so on.

None of this data quite fits in your date book. And you already know that scraps of paper are a losing formula. Many successful people keep a separate notebook for just this kind of information. They know that they will have to look in only one place to find their notes, no matter what the topic. When the notebook is full, they put it on a bookshelf where they can always go back to it, and start another notebook. Each time you start a notebook, put the beginning date on the cover; when it's full, add the ending date.

Keep it simple revisited

At the beginning of every school year, I would come up with the most detailed system of time management. I'd schedule every minute of my day, take notes on every word the teacher said in every class, come home and recopy my notes, and study four hours every night. I would follow this plan religiously for about two weeks, then mess up one day. Suddenly, I'd go from total plan to no plan, like someone on an extreme diet who cannot recover after one lapse.

Make a reasonable plan that you can realistically stick to. Schedule time when you can do anything you want and feel good about it, rather than guilty. If you see your date book as a tool to help you get the most out of life, you will want to act on what you've written down.

Staying organized

Remember, getting organized and staying organized is a lifelong effort, but well worth it. If you lapse, don't give up, any more than you would if you made a bad pass or took a hurdle off the wrong foot. Keep working to improve your organizational skills. Learn to be effective even though you are under pressure, just as you would in your sport. Pressure is part of the definition of life.

CHAPTER 8

SELECT THE RIGHT COLLEGE AND THE RIGHT COACH

Being recruited to play sports in college is a status symbol, like having the right sneakers. "Are you being recruited?" "Yeah!" Well, we hate to burst your bubble—but recruiters are not fat guys with red suits and white beards, carrying bags full of athletic scholarships. Recruiters may care about you as a person, but their *job* is to sign up athletes who will help their teams win.

From your point of view, "selecting the right college" is what it's all about. You—not the college recruiters—must decide which college to attend. Recruiters will show interest only if you can contribute to their programs. But it's up to you to select a college that serves your best interests at the same time. In the hoopla surrounding recruiting, it's easy to lose sight of this fundamental point.

You may be a high school superstar who is actively recruited by big-time colleges. Or, you may want to continue your sport in college even though you're among the majority of athletes who won't ever make the cover of *Sports Illustrated*. Perhaps you are already a student in a 2-year college and want to transfer to a 4-year college. No matter what your situation, the information in this chapter will help you achieve your goals.

Look, mom, no athletics!

Pick a school you would like even if there were no sports. That's what dozens of athletes and coaches told us when we asked them, "What advice about selecting a college would you give to your son or daughter?"

The biggest mistake you could make in selecting a college would be to ignore this advice. Things can change quickly in your sport. The coach could leave. You could be injured. Another athlete could take your spot. Suddenly you find yourself out of competitive athletics, at a college you selected only for its athletic program. You look around and discover you hate the place. Socially and academically, it's not the college for you. And if you transfer to another college, the NCAA may punish you with severe loss of eligibility, and the college may not accept some of your hard-earned credits.

Which college do I want to attend?

You can ask yourself questions to help figure out the best college for you, and to screen out colleges that don't meet your needs. Add your own questions to the ones on our list, which were suggested by college athletes and coaches. Focus on the questions that will help you the most. Don't get lost in the details.

These questions are in three categories: athletic, academic and career, and social. Balance all three of these categories to come up with the best mix for you.

Most of these questions are easy to answer. With some, it's not always obvious how to find the answer. Later on, we'll give you some ideas on how to go about it. In every case, the first step is to ask.

JUST ASK QUESTIONS!

Athletics questions

- Is the system right for me? Will I fit in with the team's strategy, or will I be like a passing quarterback in a running offense?

- Will I be comfortable with the coach's approach to practicing?

- What about the coach's approach to discipline?

- Will I be able to develop my athletic ability as fully as possible in this program?

- How does my ability compare to this school's program? Do I want to be in a big-time program even if I may not start or star, or do I want to be a top performer on a lower level team?

- When recruiting, do representatives of this college one-sidedly praise my athletic ability, or make promises about playing time and about not recruiting other athletes at my position? Should I believe these promises?

- Do they say that their program will increase my chances for a pro career? How do I feel about that as a recruiting technique?

- Will I be happy at this college if the coach leaves?

- Is this school under investigation for possible violations of NCAA rules? If so, what are the probable outcomes, and when? How might that affect me?

- How long has the coach been at the school? Under what circumstances did the coach leave his or her previous job? Fired? Accepted a better job?

- What is the coach's win-loss record? What are this college's expectations about winning? If the team doesn't win, will the coach be fired?

- How much turnover is there among assistant coaches?

- Has the coach ever not renewed an athletic scholarship solely because of poor performance or injury?

Academics and career questions

- What is the right major for me? Does this college have a department in that major that will suit my needs?

- Is the academic level at this college too demanding for me? Will I be in over my head? Or is it too easy, not challenging enough?

- Does this school accept athletes who meet the NCAA minimums for eligibility, or are their requirements stiffer?

- Does the coaching staff believe that academics are important or just something that may get in the way of eligibility? What happens if pressure to win conflicts with educational demands?

- Will this college evaluate my academic level? If I need courses to get up to speed, are they available?

- Is tutoring available for athletes? Are there required study periods? If so, is that something I want?

- What is the graduation rate among scholarship athletes in my sport?

- How well prepared are graduates for careers? Does the school keep athletes eligible with non-challenging majors that do not prepare them to compete in the world beyond sports?

- Do former team members have good jobs? Are they advancing in their careers?

Social questions

- Do I want to be in a college located near home? Or do I want to go somewhere different? Is there a particular area or climate I'd like?

- Do I want to be in a big city? Or on a campus with a beautiful natural setting?

- What is the makeup of the general student body—economically, ethnically, geographically? Will I be comfortable here?

- What about the people on the team? Are they people I'd select as friends?

- How many students attend this college? Would I be more comfortable in a small college, where there may be more individual attention? Or do I want the resources, activities, and diversity that a big college may offer? Is there a way to get individual attention even if the college is large?

- Are the students at this college mainly into athletics? partying? studying? religion? Or does it depend on whom you hang out with?

- How do athletes and the other students get along? Are they isolated from each other or is there lots of interaction?

- How much will it cost to attend this school, beyond my athletic scholarship or whatever other financial aid I'm receiving? What are the indirect expenses, such as transportation and spending money?

You can search for the perfect college, but you won't find it

Now that you've answered all the questions, you can picture a college that has everything you want. In real life, there is no such college. Each college will have some features you like and some you don't. There's no point in trying to match a college to your every preference. Find a college that you are comfortable with.

Divide what you're looking for into three areas

To select the best college for you, divide what you want into three areas. Figure out what you *must have*, and what *would be nice*, but doesn't matter all that much. Between those extremes, put features that are *important*, but you could live without. Make a list of the items in each category. Rule out any college that doesn't have all your "must haves." Then, consider your "importants." Finally, look at the "would be nices."

Here's an example of this approach, used by senior basketball sensation Joe Shott. Joe is one of the most highly recruited high

THE MAGIC CARPET RIDE
OF RECRUITING

© 1999 AthleteNetwork.com

school basketball players in the country, and there has been a lot of speculation about which college will win his services.

When Joe started thinking about where to go to school, TV exposure was the main thing on his mind. He wanted to be on a team with lots of nationally televised games, so millions of people could catch his act. He wanted a team with cool uniforms, so he'd dazzle all his high school buddies. He saw himself going to the NBA after his sophomore season.

In ninth grade, basketball was all Joe could think about. In eleventh grade, Joe blew out his knee. For the first time, playing basketball was not part of his life. While Joe was recovering, his English teacher turned him on to the world beyond basketball. He got excited about reading and writing. The English teacher sponsored a club that produced videotapes. Joe got into that too. It was fun to do and fun to learn more about. Over time, Joe saw the problem in holding out for a dream that might or might not come true. He did not want to be left out in the cold if he didn't make it as a professional athlete. He saw that an athletic scholarship was an opportunity to get a free college education. At the same time, if everything worked out, he could have a legitimate chance to play in the NBA. Joe decided to prepare himself for a career in communications, as well as working toward becoming a professional basketball player. He developed this picture of an ideal college.

Joe Shott's ideal college

Must haves
- a good communications major
- a Division-I basketball team that likes to run
- a top-20 team with a strong chance to make it to the Final Four
- a head coach who believes in academics and thinks that good students tend to be smart about basketball too

Importants
- a large university, where athletes and non-athletes mix
- a team that recruits nationally and internationally (Joe lived in one neighborhood all his life, and wants to meet a wide range of people.)
- a chance to start as a freshman

Would be nices
- near mountains and seacoast (Joe has always lived in a flat inland area.)
- in or near a big city
- near where Joe's aunt (a great cook) lives
- lots of televised games, cool uniforms

Joe compared South Coast State University to this list. SCSU has all of his "must haves." The college is known for its fast-break style of basketball. It's also widely respected for its communications department. SCSU has two of Joe's three "importants." He probably won't be able to start as a freshman. There is a senior who starts at his position who will almost certainly be picked in the first round of the NBA draft. SCSU's coach expects that Joe would start for the three years after that. As for Joe's "would be nices," South Coast, as its name suggests, is near the ocean, but nowhere near mountains. There is a big city, where Aunt Susan lives, but it's 90 miles away. There are lots of televised games, and an endless supply of Mercury shoes and clothes.

South Coast compared well to his ideal picture, so Joe put the school on his "short list" of three or four colleges from which he'll make his final choice. It's good to see that one of Joe's "must haves" shows that he wants a strong education in communications, which could lead to a career after basketball. Another shows that he wants a coach who supports that goal. Joe hopes to get into the NBA, but he realizes that he has to prepare himself for an alternative.

Selecting the right college
starts with success in high school

Joe's ideal picture did not include items such as remedial courses or tutoring. That's because Joe got good advice (much of which was right out of this book) from his English teacher. Joe applied himself to doing well in school. He expects to apply the same discipline to academics in college, which he knows from his older sister will be harder.

Make a realistic assessment
of your athletic ability

It's tough to be objective about your own ability. Most people overestimate or underestimate their talent. Your best bet is to ask others, "Based on my ability, what colleges do you think would offer me athletic scholarships?" Ask people who are knowledgeable about you and your sport, whose judgment you respect, and who have nothing riding on the outcome. Your high school coach and opposing coaches might fit this description. Ask enough people so that you won't be overly influenced by one strong, but incorrect, opinion. Learn how to listen. If your high-school coach says, "I think you will be the number-1 point guard on South Coast State's list," his opinion is that they will offer you a scholarship. If he says, "Well, there's always a chance that SCSU will recruit you," he's trying not to hurt your feelings, but his opinion is—they won't.

Make a realistic assessment
of your academic ability

Academic success at any college requires consistent hard work. You can help yourself by selecting a college that will encourage your efforts. For example, if schoolwork remains a struggle for you, an athletic scholarship to a college where most of the students come from the top 10% of their high school class might not be in your best interests. If you discourage easily, pick a college where the athletic program supports a structured academic environment. You want a program that insists that you go to study hall, that makes it easy to get assistance from tutors, that doesn't wait for you to fail and then say, "Bye-bye." If you are strong academically, select a school that will challenge you and that has a strong department in your area of interest.

Create a short list

Use the assessments of your athletic and academic ability when you put together your list of five or six colleges to seriously consider. You might want to take an approach which has worked well for many athletes. List two colleges where the program is right at your level, two where you think you're reaching a bit, and two you're certain you can count on for scholarship offers. That way, you'll be sure to get a scholarship, and you'll have a chance to get into the best school possible.

Be sure the college wants you

All the coaches who were talking to Joe Shott wanted to sign him up, but that's not the case with every athlete. Be sure to ask if a coach is offering you an athletic scholarship. You want to know that at least two of the schools on your list of five or six will give you a scholarship. There is no point in making a list of colleges if none of them want you.

Graduation rates are published

Each year, the NCAA publishes information about graduation rates from athletic programs of all Division I, II, and III colleges. This information is sent to high schools, and Division I and II college recruiters are required to give it to you or your parents when you ask for it. Even if you don't ask for it, they are required to give it to you not later than the day before you are offered admission or financial aid.

Select the right coach

You will be under the supervision of a college coach for four or five years. That coach will probably have more impact on your life than any professor or friend. A coach can make your experience enjoyable, stimulating, rewarding...or miserable. How can you find the right coach?

There is no perfect coach. Of course you want a coach who can help you improve your athletic performance. Just don't stop there.

Select a coach you're comfortable with. If you're having a problem, if things aren't going as you expected, you want to be able to talk to your coach. Find a coach whose values you share, and whose personality fits with yours—someone you respect and will enjoy spending time with. You want a coach who cares about you as a person, not just as an athlete.

One size does not fit all

What qualities in a coach are best for you? Some coaches are strict disciplinarians, others are more easy going. Some coaches cultivate close relationships with their athletes, others keep their distance. There is no one method that will work for every athlete. In fact, some coaches vary their style in their efforts to get the most out of each player. A coach may have to speak sharply to one athlete just to be heard, while another might be crushed by the same approach. Basketball player Grant Hill is now a star for the Detroit Pistons. When he arrived at Duke as a freshman, he didn't believe he had the talent to compete at the highest collegiate level. So Duke coach Mike Krzyzewski would say, "Grant, you're doing great, you can play." Coach K even involved Hill's peers in building his morale. Christian Laettner, then a senior, who became College Player of the Year, would say, "Grant, you're the most talented player on the team."

An impartial coach doesn't necessarily treat everyone the same. He or she has the athletes' best interests at heart and figures out how to motivate them. That requires being approachable and listening. John Wooden listened to his athletes even about basketball. When they disagreed with him, he was usually right, based on his greater experience. But once in a while even Coach Wooden learned valuable lessons from his players.

If the assistant coach is your best friend, be careful

Are you tempted to go to a college because you like the assistant coach who is recruiting you and you want to continue that relationship? In some cases, you may be able to. But some assistant coaches are salespersons, constantly on the road recruiting athletes. Find out how much time your recruiter spends with the team.

A good coach can make all the difference

Kelly Hughes played volleyball in college. Like many of us she had never been an academic whiz, but she knew that education had to be her number-1 priority. So she studied hard. She also wanted to have something that at least resembled a normal college experience, even though she was focused on academics and sports.

Kelly never felt that she was on the same page as her coach. When she tried to have a balanced social life, he questioned her dedication to volleyball. When she chose finance as her major, he was not supportive, and implied that an easier major would leave her with more time to concentrate on volleyball.

When Kelly played well, the coach patted her on the back and cheered her on. When her game was off, so was the friendship. The coach projected the attitude that Kelly's social worth was tied to how well she played volleyball.

It seemed to Kelly that the coach was focused on winning to the exclusion of all other considerations. After Kelly had knee surgery in her sophomore year, the team doctor advised a few weeks more rest. Although the doctor explained the risks, he left the decision to Kelly, leaving her vulnerable to pressure. The coach talked about the importance of a big game against a conference rival. He said Kelly's teammates were counting on her and implied that she would be letting them down if she was unwilling to play with a little pain. Kelly did not feel comfortable, but she played. She was back under the knife three weeks later. The doctor said she returned too soon.

Even though they were accomplished volleyball players, many team members suffered from low self-esteem as a result of their treatment by the coach. He constantly made snide comments about their weight: "You're looking a little plump," or "It would be terrible to throw away a great career just because you can't lose 10 pounds." The coach's approach to motivating his athletes to lose weight included demeaning nicknames. He called one woman "Chubs." Kelly had a naturally slender build, but she saw her friends resort to drastic dieting under this pressure. Some became bulimic and one developed anorexia.

Communicating with the coach

Kelly was named to the All-Conference team all four years, but she felt miserable, and couldn't wait for each season to end. When Kelly got up the courage to talk to her teammates, she found that some of them also had doubts about the coach, but were afraid to confront a man who had won four National Championships and coached the Olympic Team. One athlete said, "Some people say he abuses us, but they just don't understand. When he screams at me I know that he wants what's best for me and the team. How can you question the results he gets?" Kelly thought about quitting or transferring, but she thought that would mean admitting her life was a failure. Today she looks back and laughs at how she measured her self-worth almost totally by the coach. Although the coach was said to run a model program, nobody kept track of the lives of his athletes after college. A few became pro stars. Many failed to graduate; many who did graduate were unprepared for a career or had physical or emotional problems.

Years later, Kelly talked to her former coach about some of these issues. His reaction: "You never once approached me with your concerns. You can't expect me to be a mind reader." To Kelly, he had seemed unapproachable, driven to win, with no time for anything other than volleyball.

When Kelly thought back to when she was being recruited, she realized she had allowed herself to slide into her unfortunate situation. When she had tried to ask questions, the coach had acted as though he was admitting her to heaven. She wasn't supposed to ask if her angel wings fit. It's unfortunate that Kelly allowed herself to be intimidated. But it's good that she eventually recognized the problem and worked to overcome it.

Kelly played pro volleyball after graduating, then worked for a sports apparel company. Being away from volleyball made Kelly realize how much it meant to her. She loved playing and studying the game when it was not turned into a grind. She loved the camaraderie and the competition. Kelly volunteered to coach volleyball at a Boys and Girls Club, and discovered she loved to teach. She became an assistant coach at a college whose head coach she respected for his dedication to developing players as all-round people. Several years later, Kelly Hughes became the head coach at South Coast State University.

Pressure to win

SCSU gave a good sales pitch on the importance of academics, but it was obvious to Coach Hughes that winning was priority number one for the boosters and administrators. When her team finished in the middle of the Conference several years in a row, Coach Hughes was criticized for refusing to offer scholarships to some top high school players even though they met the minimum NCAA standards. Coach Hughes emphasized academics and moral character as well as athletic talent. She showed her players that they could be students and athletes, and sold them on the dangers of taking shortcuts. She was highly respected by her former players, who became the program's best salespeople. They spread the word that Coach Hughes was demanding about volleyball and academics because she really cared about her athletes. Gradually her teams grew stronger and began to attract the best high school players. Not only did she graduate top students, but South Coast became a powerhouse in college volleyball—winning three championships in five years.

Success breeds increased expectations

The boosters started taking championships for granted. They'd get down on Coach Hughes if she did not win, and even expected undefeated seasons. After three top players graduated, hopes for continued success rested heavily on freshman Jill Pine, who had been one of the all-time great high school stars. Jill had gotten good grades in high school and Coach Hughes had been straightforward with her about the need to be a serious student in college. When Jill got to South Coast she applied herself—to volleyball and partying. She quickly became one of the top college volleyball players, leading her team to an undefeated season heading into the NCAA Tournament. On the day before the first Tournament game, the coach discovered that Jill had been cutting classes and not turning in assignments. She suspended Jill for the rest of the season, despite protests from boosters, fans, and other players. Number-1 ranked South Coast lost in the first round. Coach Hughes explained that under no circumstance would she compromise herself to satisfy those who care only about wins and losses. It was more important to teach Jill Pine the lesson that academics came above all else.

At first Jill was furious and wanted to quit South Coast and transfer to another school where "they're serious about volleyball." Senior team members convinced her to stay and study. Jill, now a doctor practicing sports medicine, credits Coach Hughes for turning her life around.

Pick a school you would like even if there were no sports

You say we've said this already? OK! You remembered the main principle of selecting the right college for you.

CHAPTER 9

COLLEGE ATHLETICS 101

Your high school offers no course in college athletics as a business. But to evaluate the statements and actions of the coaches and others with whom you're speaking, you need to understand the business of college athletics. It's simple, once we clear away the hype.

Rah-rah-rah

College presidents often say that the purpose of athletics at their schools is to

- give students an opportunity to be "well rounded," to develop their bodies as well as their minds, to learn competition and teamwork
- generate school spirit

Big-time football and basketball programs may well generate school spirit. They may also contribute to the well-rounded development of some of their players, although others develop only well-rounded muscles. But why do hundreds of grown men and women endlessly fill newspaper columns and TV screens with debate about which football team is number-1 in the nation? And why do some college coaches earn more than college presidents? Is it more than molding character and creating school spirit? Big-time basketball and football play a huge role in the nation's entertainment, but involve only 2% of all college athletes, and only a fraction of 1% of all college students. Why do universities sponsor these programs? How do such multimillion-dollar athletic enterprises fit into a university's academic mission?

The Big Time

College athletics includes many sports. Which is the most important? For you, it's simple. The most important sport is the one you participate in, whether it's basketball or water polo, football or field hockey.

Now put yourself in the shoes of the president or athletic director of South Coast State University. Which sports are most important to you in this role? The ones that bring in big bucks. Big-time, revenue-producing programs. Football. Men's basketball. The college sports you see on TV throughout the United States, and even throughout the world. Football and men's basketball fill stadiums and arenas with paying customers. Women's college basketball has edged onto the TV screen and has also become a revenue-producer at some schools.

A college team, big time or not, may spend money on the following:

- salaries for head coach and assistant coaches
- salaries for trainers and medical staff
- equipment
- team travel
- public relations
- administrative expenses: office, phone, fax, computer, postage, etc.
- athletic scholarships
- recruiting: salaries of recruiters, travel, athletes' visits to campus, etc.

A college team may take in money from the following:

- ticket sales
- radio broadcast rights
- TV broadcast rights
- sale of team-related merchandise
- donations from boosters (we'll talk about boosters later)

- contributions from participants and their families (for sports that don't make money and get little or no support from the college)

Now, picture, say, the cross-county team at South Coast. Plenty of money goes out. Check the "spend" list.

What money comes in? There are no ticket sales. There is no radio or TV money. SCSU pulls in a lot of money from the sale of merchandise with the college logo and name. It's the basketball and football teams, with their national TV exposure, that get people to buy SCSU shirts, jackets, caps, and mugs. People buy SCSU posters showing football and basketball players. Some SCSU sports other than basketball and football take in more money than the cross-country squad. The hockey and baseball teams, for example, gain revenue from ticket sales. But, their expenses are also higher than those of the cross-country team.

Most sports programs at SCSU or any other college are like the cross-country team. They spend more than they make. Year after year. There are only two sources from which to make up the difference:

- The college's general budget. That is, the same funds that are used to pay for academics, building maintenance, and just about everything else.
- Big-time revenue-producing sports programs.

OK, you're still wearing the shoes of South Coast's president. You are going over the budget with your Board of Trustees. Funds are tight. You want to hire more professors and create new academic programs, but you can't. SCSU is a public institution and the state government is after you to make cuts.

Not only that, you also have to find funds to expand women's sports. A 1972 federal law (known as "Title IX") requires that colleges offer opportunities in sports programs equally to women and men. Do you and the trustees want to finance the men's and women's cross country teams from the general budget? Or from big-time revenue-producing sports?

Now that you're an experienced college president, you know the answer.

The need for victories

What does the football team or the basketball team have to do to pull in as much money as possible?

Win!

Winning can be worth millions of dollars to a college. For example, a win or loss in one game can decide who is invited to a major Bowl. The payout for the 1999 Rose Bowl is $13 million per team. Talk about pressure on coaches and athletes.

Winning breeds increased expectations among fans—and athletic directors. Big-time athletic departments depend on the financial windfalls of Bowl games and NCAA tournament appearances to support all their programs. So even an excellent record, one that might be a success for a team that usually finishes near the bottom, can be a financial setback for a team that is used to winning.

Losing can turn a big-time revenue-producing program into a big-time revenue-losing program. The SCSU football team has huge expenses, including chartering airplanes and overnight stays in luxurious hotels for over a hundred people. Several losing seasons in a row can be a financial disaster for SCSU. Just when the payouts from Bowl appearances disappear, boosters' contributions dry up and shoe companies reduce their support. It gets ugly: Callers to sports radio shows demand that the coach be fired, and insult players by name. As an athlete, it's important to get a feel for the situation you're getting into. Some athletes thrive in a pressure cooker, others enjoy their sport more when big bucks are not riding on the outcome.

Winning = more $$$$

Maybe winning and money shouldn't be tied together, but they are.

Why is winning so critical to generating income? Think about the sources of money. People buy more tickets—and they'll pay more for those tickets—to see a winning team. More people watch winning teams on TV. Those are the games TV stations and networks want, because they can deliver more viewers to advertisers, and therefore charge advertisers more. So colleges with winning programs get the most radio and TV money. Football teams that get into Bowl games and basketball teams that are invited to the NCAA's "Big Dance" make bundles of extra money from tickets, TV, and radio.

One of the biggest sources of funds for college athletic programs is the sale of team-related merchandise: T-shirts, sweatshirts, jackets, caps, posters, pictures, calendars, mugs. People want to identify with winners, so when teams win, sales increase. When a superstar player sets records, sales of merchandise with that player's number also set records. Just take a look at what people are wearing and at what's available in the stores.

How much money are we talking about?

CBS paid one billion dollars in 1989 for the rights for seven years to broadcast the annual NCAA basketball tournament. But it wasn't enough! As the tournament grew in popularity, the rights increased in value. So CBS held off the competition by negotiating a new agreement with the NCAA. The new agreement, for the eight years from 1995 through 2002, is for $1.725 billion. That's $216 million each year. Along with the rights to broadcast the "Road to the Final Four," CBS also gets the NCAA baseball finals, the outdoor track championships, women's gymnastics, and the Division II men's basketball final game.

How much is $1.725 billion? In numbers, it's $1,725,000,000. If you made $1 million every year, it would take you 1,725 years to make $1.725 billion. But wait, there's more. There's ESPN, which played such a huge role in making college basketball what it is today. The NCAA signed a new contract with ESPN in 1994. That one covers the women's NCAA basketball tournament and championship matches in a number of other sports. The millions of dollars from this contract go directly to the colleges through their athletic conferences.

There's still more TV revenue, from all the regular season football games, the Bowl games, and the regular season men's and women's basketball games. College sports are also shown on ABC, NBC, and on hundreds of cable channels. But it doesn't stop there.

Think of 40,000, 50,000, or even 100,000 people buying tickets to college football games. And of the crowds of 10,000, 15,000, and 20,000 that pay their way into arenas to watch college basketball night after night.

And that's just the ticket revenue.

In 1996, colleges collected royalties on over $2.5 billion in sales of sports-related licensed merchandise. Carl Watson, South Coast's shooting guard, is college basketball's premier player. NBA superscout Buddy Lee describes Carl as "Michael Jordan— but with a better jump shot." SCSU generates huge revenues from apparel bearing Watson's #4. Carl's jersey was the second biggest money-maker among all licensed sports apparel, professional and college. Only Michael Jordan sold more jerseys. Unlike Michael, Carl could not receive a penny from these sales.

Who gets the money generated by college sports?

Billions go to the colleges; additional billions go elsewhere. Television networks pay huge sums to broadcast college games, but they collect even more from advertisers. Manufacturers of clothing pay colleges for the use of their names and logos, but make more from retail stores, who in turn make more from sales to the public. The NCAA takes its cut from the deals for the championships it sponsors. Many individuals ultimately end up receiving part of this income as salaries: NCAA officials, manufacturing and retail executives, TV and radio producers, directors, announcers, commentators, statisticians, engineers, camera operators, and many others.

Who ends up receiving the billions that go to the colleges? Athletic directors, coaches, assistant coaches, trainers, groundskeepers, secretaries, clerks, public relations people, equipment manufacturers, transportation providers, and many others. Some goes for athletic scholarships. That's the only part of this income stream that college athletes are permitted to touch.

What makes coaches tick?

There's pressure on Babe Steele, SCSU's head basketball coach, to continue winning so the big bucks keep rolling in. If SCSU doesn't win, the trustees, the president, the athletic director, and the boosters will be disappointed. After a few losing years, the athletic director is probably not going to say, "That's OK, Babe, we know your program is molding fine young men. It would be nice if you could win some games, but keep up the good work." He is more likely to say, "Good luck in your next job."

Keeping his job is important to Coach Steele. He and the head football coach are the highest paid employees at SCSU. Coach Steele makes more than his bosses: the athletic director, the college president, and the governor of the state. Combined. His base salary alone is $500,000, from a fund supplied by the boosters. In addition, he has a $300,000 consulting contract with Mercury Shoes. The SCSU Marauders wear Merx, which puts the company logo on TV. Coach Steele makes another $200,000 per year from product endorsements, his weekly local TV show, fees for speeches, and the basketball summer camp he conducts at SCSU. That adds up to $1 million a year.

If Coach Steele keeps winning, he can step up to even more income, perhaps to a coaching job in the NBA. If he loses, it can be a big step down. It's not just the money. His kids are happy in the local high school, his wife has a good job and doesn't want to move, and he likes the college and the staff he has put together. After winning the national championship last year, Coach Steele is treated like a god. If he starts losing, he is demoted from that heavenly position. In fact, the community leaders will want to run him out of town.

Money isn't everything

Coaches in other sports are often under similar pressures. While the biggest money is in basketball and football, winning in any sport can result in advancing to a better job, running a summer camp, coaching in the Olympics, getting endorsement deals, consulting contracts, speaking engagements, and opportunities to write articles and books.

For many coaches, money isn't the main consideration. Most coaches are former athletes. They are competitors who enjoy winning and seeing their athletes win. Winning is fun. Of course, many coaches are believers in Coach Wooden's doctrine that winning means giving your all, regardless of the score. Coach Steele gets upset after a victory if his team played poorly and praises his players after a defeat if they played well.

But the college president is looking for victories. When it comes to squeezing more money out of the state government, it's victories that count, not effort. So Coach Steele needs the team to win. Of course, he's playing against teams whose coaches are also driven to win. They can't all win. Every time SCSU wins, the other team loses. There will be only one champion in the conference. Over 300 men's Division I basketball teams compete for the NCAA Championship. Only 36 football teams will go to Bowl games, and half of them lose.

"Play here and I'll make you the next Michael Jordan"

What does a coach do to win? Two things. Recruit the best athletes and coach them as well as possible.

Which is more important? Everyone agrees that no coach, no matter how great, can win without the "horses." If the opponents' linemen are bigger, stronger, and faster, SCSU probably won't win many football games. If the starting five on opposing basketball teams average three inches taller than SCSU's starting five, and play just as well, Coach Steele will probably have a losing season.

OK. Coach Steele and his recruiting staff are competing for the best high school players. What will they do to get them?

Just yesterday, a prospect told Coach Steele that a recruiter from rival North Coast said, "We'll make you the focal point of our offense and showcase you for the NBA."

Coach Steele believes the last thing this athlete needs is another boost to his ego, which has been inflated by years of adulation. He wants to tell him, "You're not as good as they've built you up to be. You have a lot of potential, but if you don't

© 1999 AthleteNetwork.com

work hard you're going to be a bust." Coach Steele wants to say that, but does he take the risk of losing the prospect? Some athletes see it as a sign of respect when a recruiter tells it like it is. But maybe this kid isn't one of those. Should that affect the coach's decision?

The word on the street is that NCSU brings in athletes who don't belong academically and somehow keeps them eligible. There are rumors about cash payments, assignments completed by other students, and SATs taken by ringers. But among the general public, NCSU's reputation is still good.

Coach Steele hates this, because it is not in the athletes' best interest. Does he have to get into this gutter anyway? Can he win if he doesn't? Stay tuned.

OK, a recruiter is in your house

Will he tell it like it is or tell you what you want to hear? Do you think he might stress the benefits of his program and omit the drawbacks? For example, will he talk about the great uniforms and the large crowds, and leave out that the school is under investigation by the NCAA and may face suspension from post-season play for the next two years? Or that the graduation rate from their program is lower than that of other schools you are considering? The recruiter is out to sell a program. That's his job. Selecting a college that meets your needs is your job.

CHAPTER 10

MORE PLAYERS IN THE RECRUITING GAME

"College Athletics 101" gave you the big picture. There are some details to fill in. We've talked about what motivates coaches. Let's add a few words about the role of the other key players: assistant coaches, boosters, high school coaches, and "street agents." Let's also consider another group of involved people: your parents, your brothers and sisters, your friends, and you.

Assistant coaches

Assistant coaches have the same basic motivation as head coaches. They want to create a winning program. That's their ticket to keeping their job and to advancing their careers.

Big-time football and basketball programs and some other programs have "assistant coaches" whose main job is recruiting, not coaching. These assistants locate potential recruits in junior high school or early in their high school careers. NCAA regulations prohibit Division I coaches or assistant coaches from contacting you before July 1 of your junior year in high school. In football, the date is August 15. They can come to high school practices or games; they can watch you; but they are not allowed to talk to you in person or by phone or to write to you. Somehow, they manage to make it known they are interested. The assistant coaches assigned to recruiting want to build relationships with athletes to help sell their programs.

The head coach sets the tone for every program, determines who plays, and defines the program's attitude toward academics. So in evaluating a program an athlete should place a lot of weight on the character, personality, and approach of the head coach.

In some sports, an athlete will be spending a lot of time with one assistant coach. Football has more assistant coaches than any other sport. There are offensive and defensive coordinators, special teams coaches, quarterback coaches, line coaches, and more. If you are going be under the direct supervision of an assistant, evaluate that assistant as well as the head coach.

Boosters

Boosters are well-to-do people who like to be involved with a team. They contribute money, goods, or services to their teams. Some boosters are graduates of the college whose team they support, others are not.

Some boosters like to know who is being recruited, and may act independently of the coach. NCAA regulations limit the extent to which boosters can be involved in recruiting. (See the *NCAA Guide for the College-Bound Student-Athlete*.) But some "friends of the program" get around the rules by not registering as boosters. In Division I, according to NCAA regulations, boosters are prohibited from contacting potential recruits. In Division II boosters can write to you or call you after September 1 of your junior year in high school, but may not contact you in person. Division III boosters can contact you in person after your junior year.

An exception to this ban is if the contact is "part of a college's regular admissions program for all prospective students, including non-athletes." How many boosters do you suppose are out pursuing the "next Albert Einstein"?

High school coaches

High school coaches are in a position to influence college selection:

- They have a close relationship with their athletes.
- They may have influence with an athlete's parents.

- Contacts by college coaches are limited by the NCAA; the high school coach is there every day.

Many high school coaches love their athletes and truly have their best interests at heart. They've been through the recruiting process many times, helping to put limits on recruiters so that athletes can focus on their senior year. Your coach may therefore be an excellent source of advice for you and your parents.

However, you've got to follow the "Don't believe everything you hear" rule. With the best intentions, the coach may have incomplete information. Or he or she may be biased, or may have something to gain from leading you toward one college over another. Steering an athlete toward a college might help a high school coach land consideration for a college job, a summer camp coaching assignment, or some other reward.

Street agents

People do not call themselves "street agents," as it is not a flattering term. Street agents act as go-betweens. They have unofficial relationships with colleges and with high school athletes. Street agents closely follow high school sports, regardless of what else they may do for a living. They may be coaches in summer leagues, AAU coaches, executives of athletic shoe companies, business people, professionals, or factory workers, or they may have no visible means of support. Street agents are likely to have ulterior motives for recommending a college. Be sure to carefully compare the college a street agent recommends to your ideal picture.

Parents

We'll use the word "parent" or "parents" to stand for your mother, your father, or anyone else who is acting as your parent.

Your parents know you well, and understand your strengths and weaknesses. They can help you big time when it comes to selecting a college. To take advantage of their help, you've got to be open with your parents about what you are looking for in a college.

Listen to your parents' advice, but test it. Ask why. Do they

© 1999 AthleteNetwork.com

want you to go to a particular college because they were impressed by the coach, or because they have really thought through why it's the best school for you? Are they giving too much weight to a college because it's the one they went to? Are they ruling out colleges far away, because they can't bear to part with their son or daughter? Or are they ruling out colleges close by?! Do they understand your ideal picture of a college? Have you told them?

One thing your parents may be able to do well is to act as a buffer between you and a recruiter. You may be more comfortable if your parents ask some of the tough questions.

Older brothers, sisters and friends

If you are fortunate enough to have an older relative or friend who is selecting a college, you can learn by watching that process. Follow up by talking to him or her about how the college worked out. If your relative or friend is an athlete, fine. If not, better yet. You'll learn how to select a school for academic and social reasons.

Apply your relative or friend's experience to your needs. What's right for him or her may not be right for you.

Teammates

Talking over your choices with your teammates can be valuable. Some of them will be selecting colleges at the same time, so you can compare notes and toss around ideas. That's a big plus. Try not to jump to a conclusion based on something a friend says—it may be only one part of a complex picture. You might end up changing your mind from day to day as other parts of the picture jump into focus. If a close friend has a strong opinion, consider it carefully, but don't feel you have to accept it.

You

You're the most important player in the recruiting game because it's your life. When all is said and done, the decision about where to spend the next four years is up to you. You may be limited by what school will accept you. But that's based largely on what you accomplished athletically and academically in high school.

HALFTIME

by Ann Meyers Drysdale

I come from a family of eleven kids. Basketball, baseball, football, and track were as natural in our family as eating and sleeping. Our father, who had played basketball at Marquette University, loved sports and was always teaching us something: how to dribble, serve a tennis ball, high jump, swim. My sister Patty, the first child and an athlete and family leader, also helped create this wonderful, confidence-building environment. I tried to emulate my brother Dave, who is two years older than me, both as a basketball player (he played in the NBA) and as a person (he's a really good guy). We were all competitive—with eleven children, what else could you be? Sports showed us that teamwork led to success. Funny thing: to compete you had to cooperate.

We also learned to play by the rules. No way were your brothers and sisters going to let you cheat. Losing was bad, but you could feel good about how you played, and you could come back and win the next day. We learned to tell the truth and respect ourselves and our opponents. To get better you had to work, especially when your older brothers and sisters were bigger, stronger, and faster. Same thing in the classroom: to do well, you had to crack the books, not look for a way to get by with the minimum.

Our Mom, who is still generous and giving, ran an open house. We'd bring friends home with us—often whole teams. Many of our friends knew that if you needed an adult to listen and help you figure things out, Mom was there for you. (And she'd feed you.)

Our parents were not pushovers. Each of us had chores to do: dust, vacuum, wash cars, pull weeds, put laundry away. We'd go out and play until it was dark, but our homework had to be done first.

Everybody join in

Teamwork, healthy competition, and respect carried over from sports to the rest of our family life. It turns out that what was true for our family is true for the larger society. Drug and alcohol abuse and dropping out are huge problems in high schools today. As a group, young athletes, male and female, do better than other students, despite the publicity when an individual athlete messes up. According to a published study, girls participating in sports have higher self-esteem, are 92% less likely to be involved with drugs, 80% less likely to have unwanted pregnancies, and three times more likely to graduate from high school.

My sisters and I realize now that we were unusual for the 1960s and 70s, before the upsurge in girls' and women's athletics. People probably called us tomboys, but our Dad and our five brothers saw us as fellow athletes. They just wanted to choose up sides and play ball. When I was in elementary school I ran track, which was the only organized sport available to girls in our area. Now, Title IX has been instrumental in opening the way for millions of girls to grow physically, mentally, and emotionally through sports.

When we played organized sports, our parents and brothers and sisters were a big group of fans. My brother David played basketball for Coach John Wooden at UCLA. I arrived at UCLA in 1975, when David was a senior and had played on two NCAA championship teams. He went on to play in the NBA for five years. I was lucky enough to become close to Coach Wooden, or "Papa" as I still call him. I think a lot about Papa's definition of success, and try to teach it to my children. Success is "Doing your best to become the best you are capable of becoming." This definition doesn't say anything about wins and losses, fame, or money, yet it led Coach Wooden to 10 NCAA Championships. Almost every one of Papa's players graduated and went on to a live a useful, rewarding life.

Sports creates communities

Kenny Washington, an outstanding player for Papa, was my freshman coach at UCLA. When classes were over for the day, I'd sit in Pauley Pavilion, watch Papa's practices, and do my homework. Then we'd practice, using the same drills. In my senior year, my coach was Billie Moore. Patty had played on Coach

Moore's national championship team in 1970 at Cal State Fullerton. Billie Moore coached our Olympic Team to a silver medal in 1976, and led our UCLA team to the National Championship in 1978.

Many people looked at me—a female athlete in the 1970s—as if I had come out of nowhere. I didn't see it that way, because of my family background plus reading. Books were big in my life. In the third grade I read about Babe Didrickson and Wilma Rudolf and thought, "I want to be like them." There was discrimination against women in sports, but some women overcame it. Athletes today who complain about the lack of female role models would be better off going to the library and finding them.

In the spring of 1978 I was drafted by the Houston Angels of the newly formed Women's Basketball League (WBL). But I needed more credits to graduate. I had used up my college eligibility, and playing in the first year of women's professional basketball tempted me. Nevertheless, I took the advice of people who cared about me, stayed at UCLA, and graduated. That turned out to be more important than I realized at the time. In my senior year I took a class in broadcasting from a great teacher, Art Freidman. His class opened my eyes to the possibility of a career in broadcasting. There were already a few female sports broadcasters. One of them was Donna de Varona, who had been an Olympic swimmer.

The Indiana Pacers signed me as a free agent and gave me a tryout. I didn't make the team—wouldn't that have been something?—but they hired me as a broadcaster, and I did about 12 Pacer games. I was only 24, and I wanted to continue as an athlete. The Pacers agreed to release me from my contract so I could play in the WBL for the New Jersey Gems. Except for that brief interlude, I've been a sports broadcaster for 18 years. In 1997 I was asked to play in the WNBA. It's great to still be thought of as an athlete, but I'm the mother of three young children and I did not want to commit to that degree of traveling. As a broadcaster of WNBA games, I can keep my commitments to my kids and still enjoy being part of women's professional basketball.

The legacy of Don Drysdale

I've had a great life, but, like everyone else, I've had my share of adversity. In 1983, my little sister Kelly, who had been a Little League star and went to Pepperdine on a basketball scholarship, was killed in a car accident. It was painful for our family to deal with this loss, but it's an article of faith with us that no matter how unfair or even tragic life is, we have no choice but to pick ourselves up and go on.

Ten years later my husband, Don Drysdale, a broadcaster for the Los Angeles Dodgers, went with the team to Montreal. He died there of a heart attack on July 3, 1993. We had been married for seven years, and had three small children. After Don's death, I cried a lot, for a long time. An outpouring of support from my family and my sports family, and the need to be there for our kids, helped pull me through.

People sometimes ask me for advice on dealing with tragedy. I don't think there is any one right way. Each individual has to find a way that works for them. We all need support, whether it's from family, friends, or organized support groups. I am very conscious that the time Don and I had together was precious. When I am together with my kids, family, and friends, I remind myself just how precious these moments are, and that we should never take each other for granted.

One of the qualities I most admired about Don was his respect for people. He cared about people, and it had nothing to do with their position in society. He treated everyone with respect, and he wanted to be treated with respect. When Don gave you his word, that meant everything. He was a fierce competitor, yet at the same time he was a good sport. He loved and respected the game of baseball, but he had a sense of perspective. He knew that ultimately it's just a game. Don was a wonderful husband and father, and it is important to me to keep his memory alive. When I teach my kids that learning and growing from sports are more significant than winning championships, I know I'm passing on Don's legacy.

The Dodgers have included us, and become part of our extended sports family, which helps my kids know who their Dad was. We'll go to Dodger Stadium and Don, Jr. and Darren will tell me, "See ya." They'll go hang out in the broadcast booth and in the clubhouse with the players.

Working together

No matter what you're doing, even if it's something as intense and competitive as sports, the most important thing in your life is other people. Don't take them for granted. Cherish them. Our athletic careers last a relatively short time, but ties with other people can last a lifetime. When I was young, most of the mistakes I made had something to do with being stubborn and not listening to the people who cared for me—parents, brothers and sisters, teachers, coaches. I usually paid the price. All this has made me a better and smarter person. Everybody has to deal with trial and error in their lives, but what helps most is when you have people who can help you in these situations. Often times it's a matter of reaching out to family and friends and letting them know you value and welcome their advice.

Now that I'm a Mom, I see how important it is to take the time to explain things. Sometimes I'm guilty of just telling my kids what to do. When they ask why, I want to say, "because I told you so." But young people need to understand why. If there really is no time, a better answer would be, "You need to do this now, and I promise I'll explain it later." Then keep your promise. It's so important to spend time with your kids and give them the attention they'd like to have from you because that moment can never be recaptured.

The sports community has been a source of support, friendship, comfort, and inspiration to me. AthleteNetwork.com is an electronic-age extension of this community. This book and the Web site can help you get the most out of sports, school, and life.

Ann Meyers Drysdale is the color analyst for the WNBA on NBC. A member of the Basketball Hall of Fame, Ann led the UCLA basketball team to the National Championship in 1978, and was named the outstanding female athlete in the country.

CHAPTER 11

CONTROL YOUR RECRUITMENT

You have a picture of the right college for you. You understand the business of recruitment. Now the challenge is to manage the recruitment process so that you make the best choice while putting the least pressure on yourself. You want to enjoy your senior year in high school.

Selecting a college is like buying a car for the first time

These days, recruiting in some sports starts as early as eighth grade. If recruiters have been after you for years, you might think you already know all the answers. Big mistake. You are up against recruiters who have been adults longer than you have been alive. If you try to outsmart them on your own, you are setting yourself up for a loss. The way to win is to take advantage of the experience of others. Winning means ending up at the right college for you.

You will probably select a college only once. That creates a problem. Normally, you learn by correcting mistakes. But when there's no second chance, you don't have that luxury.

To compound the problem, college recruiters usually have had much more experience. They've talked to hundreds of potential "customers" and made dozens of "sales."

The situation is similar to that facing first-time car buyer Maya Edwards, a hockey player at South Coast State University. As

Maya walks onto the used car lot, she is nervous and unsure what questions to ask. The cars all look attractive. Her eyes go to a red convertible that's out of her budget. She pictures herself pulling up to her friend's house in that sleek car. Maya has forgotten that she came to buy a pickup truck. The sales person recognizes the look in Maya's eyes. The next thing Maya knows, she's driving that red convertible off the lot. "How did that happen?" she asks herself as she writes a check each month for the next four years, and as she tries to cram her gear into the tiny trunk.

Think before you buy

If you were buying a car, what would you do to avoid Maya's mistakes? And how does it apply to recruiting?

Ask questions until you get answers

Maya didn't dig for the truth by asking questions. She could have asked the salesman what the interest would add to the price of the car. She could have asked him if the car was suitable for transporting gear on back roads. The salesman had no reason to volunteer this information. He didn't know her budget or that she wanted to use the car for camping trips. The salesman could have sold Maya a more suitable car by asking her about her requirements. Maya might then have become a customer for life and recommended the salesperson to her friends. Maybe the salesman didn't know any better. Or maybe he was out for the fast buck. Unfortunately, Maya's best interests were sacrificed at the same time. You may deal with recruiters who operate this way out of ignorance, greed, or just because they are in a hurry. By asking questions until you uncover the truth, you protect your interests. You also protect the recruiter from making the wrong decision and ending up with someone who won't fit in with the program or the college.

Control your ego

As an athlete, you know that when you compete, you have to concentrate on your goals. Your opponents may talk trash, the crowd may cheer or boo. You have to control your ego to avoid making a spur of the moment decision based on your emotions instead of your goals.

The salesman used Maya's ego just that way. To protect yourself from a similar approach, you might talk to people who have bought cars before. To learn everything they could teach you, you'd make a list of questions to ask them. You might bring an experienced car buyer with you to the showroom, and postpone a decision until you could consult with your advisor. That way, you'd be on a more equal basis with the salesperson. You should make an ideal picture of the car you want, and divide that into three sets of features: must haves, importants, and nices. This method is useful for selecting anything, be it a college, a job, or a jacket. Maybe even a spouse.

Coach and ballplayer strike out

Bonita Lind, a high school softball pitcher in her senior year, has attracted national attention by setting strike-out and shut-out records. Bonita is also an excellent hitter and fielder. She dreams of playing in the Olympics, which will take place when she's a junior in college. Bonita believes that focusing on raising her pitching to a higher level will make her dream a reality. She's considering going to South Coast, which plays in a conference with the top softball teams in the country.

Bonita is talking to Meg Rose, the legendary coach of the South Coast women's softball team. SCSU already has a sophomore who is a great pitcher, but the team could use more power at the plate. So Coach Rose wants to put Bonita in the outfield, where her strong arm will help the team. But Bonita doesn't think the outfield is her route to the Olympics.

Bonita asks Coach Rose if she will be able to pitch as a freshman. The Coach replies, "Sure, you'll pitch in some of our games." Meg is thinking that Bonita will be the starting pitcher in about four games, when the team's regular pitcher needs rest. But Bonita thinks "some of our games" means "about half of the games, maybe all of them." Bonita hears it that way because she wants it to be that way. Bonita doesn't request a more specific answer because she doesn't want to seem disrespectful to Meg Rose, who has coached two US Olympic teams and whose books on softball are read all over the world.

Bonita's freshman year arrives and she is in for a disappointment. So is Coach Rose. She didn't expect to have an unhappy player. Bonita is partially responsible for the miscommunication. She should have tried to nail down what the coach meant by "some of our games." Coach Rose didn't even know that Bonita's Olympic hopes were tied to pitching. If Bonita had told the coach of her desire to pitch in the Olympics, the Coach might not have given such a casual answer. In fact, she might have given Bonita the benefit of her thinking about the best way for Bonita to make the Olympic team.

Lessons of this story

- Don't be intimidated. (Easier said than done.)
- Make sure you get clear answers to your questions. Ask until you do.
- Let the coach know what is on your mind and why.
- Take advantage of every interview to learn something. Why not ask a coach, for example, what he or she thinks you should do to improve?

Good coaches welcome questions

We've blamed overzealous recruiters for many problems. But athletes and their parents are also at fault for not asking enough questions. A recruiter is not doing you a favor by talking to you. He or she believes you may benefit the team. Feel free to ask anything you want. Be open and honest. If you don't understand an answer, keep asking.

A recruiter who is thoughtful about matching his or her program to your needs will welcome your questions. If the recruiter won't give you straight answers or seems tired of your questions, you've discovered something. Do you want to attend a school where a coach appears put off by your desire to learn the facts?

Don't take candy from strangers

Sometimes agents, their employees, or others who look to benefit from your athletic ability will act as though they are concerned only with your welfare. They just happen to want to be your friend and offer you clothes, money, even a car. Or maybe they have a nice job for your Uncle Harry.

It's tough for high school and college athletes—especially those who are flat broke—to turn down these offers. They see millions of dollars going every which way in athletics—except to high school and college players.

Before you put your hand out, think about what you are doing. Many athletes violate the NCAA rules and get away with it. But if you are caught, you have to live with the consequence. Your athletic career will be over. That means you are risking a college athletic scholarship, a college education, and possibly a pro contract.

There is no Santa Claus

Even if you "get away with it," you don't. In one way or another, you owe something to those who give you money, goods, or favors. They are in it for profit. They give you what for them is chump change, with the intention of eventually collecting big time on their investment. They invest in many athletes, and profit if only a few become pros. So their risk is spread out, and any one young athlete is expendable. If you get caught, your career is over, but their profits continue.

Maintain your amateur status

If the NCAA decides you are a professional athlete, you lose your college eligibility. And there's not much of an appeals process. It's easy to become a professional athlete—as defined by the NCAA. For example, you are a pro if you are "paid (in any form) or accept the promise of pay for playing in an athletics contest." Suppose you're on a summer basketball team. The coach, a well-known street agent, pays to fly the team to the beach, and treats each player to a shopping spree in a sporting goods store he owns. Bang—you are a pro twice over. Once for the trip, once for the shopping. We know it goes on, but we want you to know what can happen if you get caught.

Another way you can become a pro before you want to is if you "use your athletics skill for pay in any form (for example, TV commercials, demonstrations)." Or if you "sign a contract or verbally commit with an agent or a professional sports organization." "Also," writes the NCAA, "receiving any benefits or gifts by you, your family or friends from a player agent would jeopardize your college eligibility." Things that are "free" often have higher price tags than things you pay for. This is especially true in those sports where ulterior motives seem to lurk.

Don't believe the hype (DBTH)

Recruiters often praise athletes to the skies, treat them to luxurious meals and accommodations, and create hoopla to influence their decisions. Real Athletes don't allow this hype to go to their heads. They keep their feet on the ground.

DBTH should be the golden rule of college recruitment.

How do you apply this golden rule? Should you buy a lie-detector and hook everybody up who tells you how great some college will be for you?

Well, who wants to drag around heavy electronic equipment? And, there are practical difficulties, such as what to do when a college coach is on the phone. Or when you're far from an electrical outlet.

Treat everybody as if they were honest

We suggest that you treat everybody as if they were honest. That way, you don't become cynical and cut yourself off from close ties with good people who care about you.

But to treat people as honest, you have to understand that things change. When a coach tells you that you are going to start as a freshman, just add in your mind, "unless someone better is available when the season starts." If a coach says that an NCAA investigation of his school won't lead to sanctions, add "unless additional evidence turns up." "You are the next Michael Jordan" means "You might be the next Michael Jordan if you develop better than 10,000 other young athletes who are also the next Michael Jordan."

If you're busy figuring out if someone is lying, it's hard to pay attention to what he or she is saying. You get distracted by trying to read facial expressions or body language. Your ego also gets involved. You might end up rejecting a good college because you thought a recruiter lied.

Treating everybody as though they were honest may seem naive. But efforts to detect lies often fail, because the best and most experienced liars come across as sincere. Treating people as honest is actually a more powerful weapon for getting at the truth. To use this method, listen carefully and ask lots of questions. Be like a trial lawyer who asks a lot of questions and discovers the "whole truth."

Are the recruiters parked outside?

When Barry Switzer was head football coach at Oklahoma University he desperately wanted to recruit Billy Sims (who went on to win the 1979 Heisman Trophy). Legend has it that Coach Switzer sent an assistant to Billy's home town with instructions not to return without Billy. Talk about recruiting pressure! The assistant checked into a nearby motel, but spent all his time with Billy and his family. He reportedly even cooked their breakfasts. The assistant was finally able to return home—and keep his job—when, after 68 days, Billy signed.

If you are a top athlete in a sport with big budgets, you will be swamped with letters, phone calls, e-mail, and personal contacts from recruiters. This attention may seem glamorous at first, but can take too much of your time. You lose effectiveness as a student and as an athlete. It becomes tough to enjoy high school. Here are some suggestions for setting limits on recruiters:

- Limit when you and your parents are available for phone calls. Instruct recruiters, for example, to phone only Tuesdays and Thursdays from 7PM to 9PM. If recruiters call at different times, politely explain when they should call.

- Limit whom you want to deal with, what you want to talk about, and how long you want to talk. For example, you can politely tell a coach or assistant coach that you are considering his or her school, but you want no calls from boosters and no calls from anybody just to chat about how well you did in your last game.

- Quickly narrow down the number of colleges you are considering by ruling out those that differ too much from your ideal picture. Once you know a college doesn't have all your "must haves," you can stop wasting time on their letters and phone calls, and you don't need to visit their campus.

How to market yourself if you are not heavily recruited

If you are among the vast majority of high school athletes, college coaches are not filling your mailbox and making your phone ring off the hook. But if you have the ability, you still may be able to get an athletic scholarship. It takes marketing! Most coaches don't have the resources to actively recruit, so you increase your chances by aggressively letting them know you are interested in their school. Plan how to make your talents known to the coaches on your list with the least expenditure of time, energy, and money.

Make a package of information about yourself that you can send to coaches. Call first to find out if a coach wants your information. You can also use this call to learn about the college.

Your package should

- explain what you can contribute to the college team
- summarize your athletic achievements
- describe how you are doing academically

Include a brief cover letter and a sheet with your height and weight and athletic and academic qualifications. You might also send photos of you participating in your sport, photocopies of clippings about your performance, and a videotape showing you in competition if that's appropriate to your sport. The tape should not be a highlight reel. A coach wants to evaluate your complete game.

Do your homework on the teams you are contacting. Then you can include something in each cover letter about why your contribution would be valuable to that team. For example, you could point out that their starter and backup in your position are graduating seniors. Or that your abilities fit in with the coach's style of play. Your package will stand out from others that are not customized. When you're a buyer, you appreciate it when the seller considers your particular needs. So when selling yourself, be sure to think about the needs of your buyer—the coach.

Of course, all your written material should be typed, and you should check for spelling, grammar, and appearance before your package goes out the door. Two sets of eyes are better than one; ask a parent or teacher to proofread. One of the worst mistakes you can make is to show carelessness by misspelling the coach's name. You're competing for a scholarship, so pay attention to every detail that can help you win. This professional approach will help you throughout your life, whether you are applying for a job or trying to sell people on your ideas.

Should you hire a recruiting agency?

Finding athletic scholarships has become big business. There has been an explosion in the number of companies selling this service to athletes and their families. Athletes who can least afford to hire these agencies are the athletes who most need scholarships. Recruiting agencies generally charge between $100 and $800, depending on what they say they are going to do. The agencies justify their fees by comparing them to the greater value of an athletic scholarship. There are several problems with this comparison:

- You pay up front, whether you get a scholarship or not.

- You might have been able to get the scholarship yourself.

Recruiting agencies say that coaches are more likely to believe their estimate of your ability than your own. According to the agencies, coaches know they will not overly praise an athlete, because the reputation of the agency would be at risk. If you prepare your own package, you can add objectivity by asking a rival coach to write a recommendation. The college coach will know that a coach from a rival high school has no personal stake in recommending you.

If you can put together a recruiting package on your own, we recommend that you do it. Coaches tell us they are more impressed by do-it-yourself efforts than by commercially produced packages.

Benefit from every phone call

You should know why you are talking to a particular recruiter at a particular time. If you have already ruled out a college, there's no reason to be on the phone with its recruiter at all. If you are still considering a college, your ideal picture is the starting point. How does this college compare? What do you still need to learn to make the comparison? Getting that information should be the goal of your phone call.

If you're like most of us, you'll remember a question you meant to ask just after you hang up. To prevent this, write down the questions that apply to this phone call, and check them off as you write down the answers. It's probably best to keep a box of note cards next to the phone, with cards for each college you are considering. You will be collecting so much information that it will become a jumble unless you write it down. If you rely on memory, you will become confused about which coach at which college said what.

There may also be information you want to bring to the recruiter's attention. Write that down too.

You want to control the phone call, but give the recruiter time to provide information to you. If it's a first contact, listen to his or her whole story. Then ask questions. Find out about all your "must haves" and "importants."

If you are shy when dealing with adults this may be hard. But the benefit of getting information that satisfies your needs is enormous, so grit your teeth and ask. Remember that you are in a powerful position. Even if the coach is a legend, he or she can't win without athletes.

After the first contact with a recruiter, listen for new information. For example, the recruiter may tell you that you are now their number-1 choice, because two athletes have signed elsewhere. Or that the college's needs have changed in some other way.

You don't have to stay on the phone while the recruiter goes over old ground or asks what your favorite food is. You can politely end the conversation at any time.

You and your parent may want to confer during a phone call. That's OK, and it's not a sign of weakness. Just tell the recruiter that you want to discuss something, and would he or she mind holding on for a minute or two.

At any time during a phone call, feel free to ask recruiters to mail you information, so that you can study it in detail. If they agree to send the information, see if they do. It's one test of how serious they are about you and about keeping their promises. Asking for information in writing is a good tactic when you feel that the recruiter is exaggerating. Jonathan Krone's father said that the North Coast State baseball coach "guaranteed" that Jonathan, a star outfielder, would be in the starting lineup as a freshman. Mr. Krone thought that was an extraordinary claim. The college had several outfielders who were not seniors, and they were trying to recruit other top high school players. So he asked the coach to put the guarantee in writing. Here's what the coach wrote: "Jonathan will start as a freshman if his performance demonstrates he is most qualified at his position."

Guaranteed.

Take advantage of home visits

The NCAA has reduced the number of times recruiters are allowed to visit your home. Therefore, recruiters usually pack all their selling points into the limited time available. Their presentations may include glossy full-color brochures and videotapes worthy of Hollywood.

Recruiting sales pitches

In the good 'ole days of recruiting, coaches gave the same presentation to everyone, like stamping cookies out of dough. Many still do. But competition for athletes has led to customized dog-and-pony shows. The coach finds out what you like and what you don't, and tries to push the right buttons to get you to sign.

Whether you're confronted with the cookie cutter or the customized presentation, ask questions to determine whether the program really meets your needs.

Control the home visit

Most of what we said about phone contacts also applies to home visits. Feel free to ask any questions you want. Prepare checklists of questions. If you have information to present to the recruiter, have notes about that as well. You are both trying to figure out if you, the athletic program, and the college will make a good fit. If the recruiter doesn't know what you are looking for, he or she is flying blind. The best recruiters will probe for this information, but others will just stick with their canned or customized presentations unless you take the lead.

Take nothing for granted. Be sure to ask, "Are you offering me an athletic scholarship?"

Negative recruiting

A recruiter using this approach tries to sign you up by knocking the opposition. Negative recruiting tells you nothing about the school the recruiter represents. You may want to listen to it, then ask a recruiter from the school under attack to respond to any points that concern you. You should not believe statements made by a recruiter about a competing school without hearing the response. And you are within your rights to cut off the negative comments by telling the recruiter you would prefer to hear about his or her program.

Campus visits:
how to dig through the snow

Did you see the movie *Blue Chips*? The coach takes three players he is recruiting into a 15,000-seat arena. They stand on the basketball court. The arena is dark, silent, empty. Suddenly spotlights sweep the floor and upbeat music fills the air. The players hear their names announced over the PA system, as though they were starting a game for Western University. What a feeling for a 17-year-old high school athlete.

Many programs try to dazzle athletes rather than give them a realistic idea of what it would be like to attend that college. One coach warns against being snowed by "a campus visit that is a 48-hour magic-carpet ride, filled with experiences that will never be part of your normal routine at the university."

Take advantage of campus visits

Meeting the team is a great opportunity, if you know how to use it.

Don't talk only to the stars or the players you are steered toward. Talk to the athletes who don't get as much playing time and to whomever you feel will be straight with you—maybe somebody you played with or against in high school. Have private conversations. Introduce yourself and explain that you are thinking of coming to this school next fall. Start with "open" questions, such as, "What has your experience here been like?" or "Could you tell me what you like and don't like about being here?" These questions are most apt to produce long responses containing lots of information. If you ask a "closed" question, such as "Do you like it here?" you are likely to get only a "Yes" or a "No." Neither tells you anything about whether you would like the school. Questions that start with "What?" "Why?" and "How?" will draw out the most information. If an athlete is unhappy with his college experience, it's not necessarily the fault of the program or the coach. See if it's an isolated incident or if you have spotted an undeniable trend. Talk to enough people to get the full picture.

On a campus visit, you will be spending time with the coaching staff and the athletes on the team. It's the best opportunity for you to get a feel for the system and the people. Are you comfortable? Will you fit in? Do you like the way the coach runs practice?

Do not waste time on a campus visit getting information that is available from other sources, such as the school catalog. Before visiting SCSU, Joe Shott told the basketball coach that he wanted to meet some of the Communications faculty and sit in on their classes. The coach included these items in Joe's schedule. By thinking ahead, Joe picked up information he could *only* have gotten from a campus visit—a first-hand impression of the Communications Department. And, he impressed the basketball coach and the professors. They see that he is a heads-up guy who takes the initiative, makes plans, and carries them out.

Campus visits: the technicalities can make you or break you

There are two ways you can visit a college campus: at your expense or at the school's. Some colleges have big budgets for financing campus visits; others don't. The NCAA has complicated rules governing college visits. Plan your visits well ahead of time so that you can use the technicalities to your advantage, rather than be tripped up by them. For example, you are limited to visiting no more than five campuses at the college's expense. So you want to be sure you go only to colleges you're seriously considering. And you must make sure your test scores and transcripts are submitted in time to allow a college to pay for your visit.

These are a few of the many rules on visits to Division I colleges in the 1998-99 *NCAA Guide for the College-Bound Student-Athlete*. The rules are different for Divisions II and III, and of course they change from year to year.

NCAA rules for visits to Division I colleges

- You can visit a college campus any time at your expense.
- During your senior year, you can accept no more than

one expense-paid (official) visit to a particular campus. You may make official visits to no more than five colleges.

- You can't make an official visit (before the first signing date in a sport that has an early signing period) unless you have given the college your high-school (or college) academic transcript and a score (it doesn't have to be a qualifying score) from a PSAT, an SAT, a PACT Plus or an ACT test taken on a national test date under national testing conditions.

Campus visits: key points

- Know the NCAA rules.
- Schedule visits way ahead of time.
- Submit your transcripts and test scores in advance.
- Visit only colleges you are seriously considering.
- Learn about the college before your trip. Use your visit to get information that's not available off campus.
- Look for the reality beneath the glitter.
- Don't accept or reject an offer of an athletic scholarship during the visit. Go home and think about it first.

The National Letter of Intent: a heavy piece of paper

What is the National Letter of Intent? The name contains three clues.

National: The same letter is used by most NCAA colleges in the United States.

Letter: It's a letter—actually a complex legal contract—that you sign to accept an athletic scholarship.

Intent: The National Letter of Intent binds you to a particular college. They don't say this in the NLI, but most lawyers agree that you are exempt in the event of your own death. Otherwise, you are stuck even if you change your mind. In the NLI you agree that if you go to another college instead, you cannot play for two years, and that you will have only two years of eligibility remaining. The letter refers to this as a "basic penalty." It sounds more like "cruel and unusual punishment." One more reason why it's so important to be serious about selecting the right college.

What's good about the NLI ?

The NLI protects colleges from each other, and protects you from continued recruiting pressures after you make a decision. Once you've signed with, say, South Coast State, other colleges will stop banging on your door.

Without the NLI, there would be no penalty against an athlete who accepted an athletic scholarship, then continued to shop around among other colleges. A college would make a commitment to an athlete, but would receive no commitment from the athlete in return.

What's bad about the NLI?

You select a college because of what it has to offer. You sign the NLI with that college. Then things change at the college, and the features that attracted you are no longer there.

Too bad. You're stuck.

What might change? The coach could leave. We hope you won't select a college based only, or even mainly, on the coach. Nevertheless, for any athlete, the coach is an important part of the equation. So you pick the coach that's right for you. Suddenly, he or she is gone. If the new coach has an approach that you don't like, too bad.

Many athletes have signed the NLI, only to be burned when a coach departs. The people who administer the NLI have responded by emphasizing that even if the coach leaves, you stay. They've put a border around NLI Article 19, so that you can't miss it.

> 19. If Coach Leaves. I understand that I have signed this NLI with the institution and not for a particular sport or individual. For example, if the coach leaves the institution or the sports program, I remain bound by the provisions of the NLI.

What other changes at the college might cause you to regret signing the NLI? The school might be found guilty of violating NCAA rules and banned from post-season play. The coach might have recruited another phenom at your position, even though he or she promised not to. There could be cuts in the academic department that attracted you.

Sign early or late?

You can sign the NLI only at designated times during your senior year in high school or your final year in junior college. Basketball has a 1-week "early signing period" in November, and a "late signing period" from early-April to mid-May. Football has one signing period, from early February to early April. Many other sports have November early signing periods and late signing periods from mid-April through July. Still others have just one signing period, from early February through July. Each year's *NCAA Guide* publishes the exact signing dates for all sports. During the late signing period, the offer is considered withdrawn if you don't sign it within 14 days of the date it was issued.

When to sign the National Letter of Intent is a tactical decision you face in the recruiting process. Should you sign early or late? If you sign late, should you sign at the beginning of the period, in April, or at the end, in July? Or if you're a football player, in early February or in late March?

Reasons for signing early

There are three reasons for accepting right away:

1) You are reasonably certain that this is the college for you.

2) You don't want to risk losing the scholarship by not accepting it.

3) You want to end the recruiting pressure and enjoy the rest of your senior year in high school or your final year in a 2-year college.

Reasons for waiting

There are three reasons for waiting:

1) The November early signing period is almost a year before you will go to college. You don't want to be locked in if things change at the college or if your needs change.

2) You think there's a good chance you'll get an offer from a college you would prefer to attend.

3) You can tolerate the recruiting pressure. It doesn't prevent you from enjoying athletics, doing your schoolwork, or preparing for your college-entrance exams.

Examples of what might change

Gary Lawrence, a highly recruited football player, was offered a scholarship at a big-time football program in the Midwest at the beginning of the signing period, in early February. Gary had never visited the college, but the coach he wanted to play for was there, and the team was a powerhouse. Gary had heard rumors that the coach was considering an NFL job and that an NCAA investigation might turn up serious violations. He asked the coach about that, and the coach said he was staying at the college and the NCAA would find that his program was clean. So Gary signed the NLI as soon as he received it.

Gary learned from sports radio station KNUT that the coach had signed a contract with an NFL team. Later that day KNUT reported that the NCAA had banned the school from Bowl appearances for two years for serious recruiting violations.

Gary still had to go to the Midwest college, even though his reasons for going were no longer valid. If Gary had waited until the end of the signing period, he could have played at other colleges. Gary, who is from sunny San Diego, will think about his mistake during the long, frigid Midwest winters.

Don't sign the NLI under the gun

A recruiter may ask you to sign the NLI during a campus or home visit. We suggest that you don't do it. Tear up the letter. Throw away the pen. The dotted line will still be there tomorrow.

Unless you've absolutely decided beforehand, signing during a visit is one of the worst recruiting mistakes you could make.

If you want to commit to a college, why not sign? Especially if the coaches tell you they are considering other athletes and their scholarship offer may be withdrawn?

Here's why. It's *possible* that the offer may be taken away within a few days, but it's not likely, especially if the coaching staff is committed to you.

On the other hand, it is *probable* that you will have second thoughts. You need a few days to recover from the hoopla. You need to compare your ideal picture of a college to this college at least one more time.

After your second thoughts, you may decide this college is best for you. That's fine. Having your second thoughts *before* making your final decision shows maturity. You will feel much better than if you had rushed into a commitment.

Verbal commitments

If signing the NLI is the worst mistake you can make during a visit, verbally agreeing to attend the college is a close second. Once you have given your word, you want to keep it. But then what do you do if you have second thoughts?

If you see or hear things during a visit that convince you not to attend the school, don't immediately say "no." After more thought, you may decide that the college looks pretty good after all. You could call back and say you changed your mind—coaches understand that young people change their minds—but why put yourself under that pressure in the first place.

So how should you respond during a visit if a coach asks you to commit? Express your appreciation for the confidence the coach is showing in you. And say you want to think about it for a few days.

Making the decision

Colleges are out to get the best athletes. They play the recruiting game in sequence: the highest rated athletes get offers first; everybody else waits. Lesser name schools also wait as athletes hold on to see if big-time programs will offer them scholarships. The game has risks for the college and the athlete.

When you're deciding whether to accept an offer, lack of intelligence can be a problem. We're talking about "intelligence" as the CIA uses the word—information about the other side. You may not know what is in a recruiter's mind. They've offered you an athletic scholarship, but how many other offers have they made? How much do they want you? Where do you stand with colleges that haven't yet made an offer, but say they are interested?

Once again, the best way to find out is to ask. If you receive an early offer from a college that is not your first choice, ask whether you are *their* first choice. You may not always get a complete answer, but you can only gain by trying. You can also call a recruiter who has not yet made an offer and explain the situation. When you have an offer from one college, it puts pressure on the other recruiter to reach a decision about you.

Will the school you want more make an offer? Will the school that has made an offer still want you later? Once you've collected as much information as you can, make an estimate. Then take a deep breath, make the decision that seems right for you, and try not to second guess yourself. Live with your decision, don't agonize over it once you can't change it. We all have to make decisions based on incomplete information. Sometimes no matter how carefully we think things through, they don't work out as well as we had hoped. But by not carefully thinking things through, we practically guarantee failure.

Deciding whether to sign early or late is one of the many decisions you have to make in selecting a college. It's good to weigh all the factors and make a tough decision. Taking control of your recruitment doesn't only help you select the right college. It also prepares you for success as a responsible adult.

Part Four
THE COLLEGE
YEARS

CHAPTER 12

SUCCESS AT COLLEGE

College is more competitive than high school academically and athletically. But there is enough time to succeed in your sport and in your studies. Stay focused and you won't be overwhelmed by it all. If you manage your time well, you can even have a social life.

No regrets

Picture yourself ten years out of college. You're 32 years old, with a spouse and two kids. You were a star in college, but like so many aspiring athletes you fell short of a pro career. Unfortunately, you didn't take academics seriously. You "majored in eligibility," had a great time, but left without a degree.

You come home tired after long hours at the wheel of a cab. That's your second job. Mornings you work as a short order cook. You've been dreading this day—your monthly bills are due. Your credit card is maxed out at $10,000, and you have utility bills and rent to pay. A red notice from the cable company claims you are delinquent on three months of service. Your bank balance is $83.72. Life sucks. You feel so helpless. What to do? You figure you can hold off the landlord a few more months. Just pay the cable bill. At least you know you can escape from the misery by watching the great late night fare. You make the minimum payment on the cable bill, and on the electricity to run it. Sitting in the cramped quarters of your mobile home, you turn to your spouse, who looks as depressed as you do, and you say, "If I had the opportunity to do it over again I would have worked my butt off in the classroom."

We don't want you ever to look back at your college days and say, "I should have," or "I would have." We want you to say, "I knew what to do and I did it."

College = opportunity

College is a great place to develop your potential.

- If you continue your sport in college, you'll be competing against the top athletes—in some cases, Olympic champions and future professionals.
- You learn to take charge. You decide what to major in, what career path to take.
- You're at a center of learning. You can take advantage of a concentration of knowledge, information, and ideas that exists nowhere else.
- You can get to know professors and students from many walks of life, and see the world from their viewpoints.

Put it all together and your opportunities for a career and a meaningful, exciting, and enjoyable life are vastly increased.

Differences between college and high school

College is not a mysterious land totally unrelated to where you've been before. The skills you learned in high school are transferable to success in college. But it's important to understand the differences between high school and college so that you're prepared to deal with them.

No roll call

Many college courses do not require attendance. You can rationalize missing classes, but it's a formula for failure. Go to every class, pay attention, take notes. You will know what the

teacher is focusing on, so you can study more effectively. Plus, it's easier to learn when you actively participate in class discussions.

More "homework"
Much more. At college, they don't call it homework. It's assigned reading, exercises, writing papers, and preparing for exams. You may need to put in two, three, or four hours a day. Consistency is the key.

Longer range assignments
Some courses have reports due weeks or months down the road. Unless you devote time each day to the necessary reading or other preparation, by the time the deadline gets near, it's too late. Most courses have midterm exams on all the material covered to that point, and final exams that cover the entire course. It's impossible to prepare for these exams by cramming a semester's worth of material into a coffee-induced all-night study bender.

Harder academic work
High school courses often inch ahead, constantly reviewing previous topics. College courses move more quickly and cover more complex material. You can cruise along pretending everything is cool—until you take the final. Then, you take an F or you let your eyes wander to the test of the A-student to your right. Either way you have failed.

Parents out of the loop
In high school, parents or guardians are expected to play a role in ensuring that you do your homework, fill out forms, pay required fees, return your library books. Each term your parents are invited to meet with your teachers to review your progress. If you are having an academic, attendance, or disciplinary problem, your parents are notified. In college, you are treated as an adult. You are responsible for your academic work and for completing all other requirements. If paperwork related to your financial aid has to be turned in by a certain date, it's up to you to make sure it's in by that date. You can say, "I didn't know," but the college holds you responsible for knowing.

Increased responsibility for daily life

For most athletes, college is the first experience living away from home. Many things you may have taken for granted become your responsibilities: housing, meals, laundry, housecleaning, paying bills, managing money, managing your time, deciding what courses to take. Even if you're still living at home while in college, you'll want the freedom and maturity that comes with taking care of your own business.

Harder work in your sport

Perhaps you got by in high school as a "natural athlete." At college, you're up against the other "naturals." You are expected to put more time and effort into mastering your sport at a higher level. With practice, conditioning, film sessions, travel, and competition it can be the equivalent of a full-time job—even if the NCAA swears it's not.

Don't pack up and go home

You wouldn't be the first person to arrive on campus and be overwhelmed. All the new and tougher things about college hit you at once. It can be hard to know what to deal with first. Some college freshmen avoid dealing with any of it. They celebrate their freedom from home by hanging out and partying. Eventually the academic requirements catch up with them. At some point, just about everyone who goes to college thinks, "This is too hard. I'm leaving." If this happens to you, remember that most students who felt that way got their acts together and went on to accomplish great things.

Prepare in high school

As with sports, the single biggest difference between winning and losing is preparation. Those who have developed good habits in high school—eating and sleeping right, a disciplined approach to studying, an interest in reading and learning—tend to do well in college. They hit the ground running. Even if they stumble, they are trained to recover.

What if you're not prepared for college?

Many students, athletes and non-athletes, arrive at college not ready to do college work. Some ignore the problem and hope it will go away. This leads to flunking out.

Other students identify their weaknesses and plug away at getting stronger. Motivation can accomplish miracles. Even students who have arrived at college illiterate have overcome the problem and done well. It just takes a lot of hard work. Deal with it. Go to community college if necessary. Take the remedial courses and special instruction you need to get you up to speed. The basic skills you need for success in college and beyond are the old three R's—reading, writing, and 'rithmetic—plus computer literacy.

Students who arrive unprepared but recognize the problem and work hard often do better than students who are complacent and think they will do well without applying themselves. Most coaches and employers will tell you that they prefer a hard working person with some ability over a person who is a natural but doesn't maximize his or her potential.

Relying on yourself

At college, without the daily support of your family, it becomes clearer that your future is up to you. In this competitive world, no one else's main task is to make sure you succeed. That's your job. Coaches, athletic advisors, teachers, tutors, family, friends will help you if you seek their help. But you are in charge of your life. What do you want? What must you do to get it? Who can help you? How will a small step today, combined with small steps tomorrow and the next day, lead to a breakthrough?

We've all heard motivational speeches that fire us up, only to find ourselves the next day sitting in front of the tube, aimlessly wasting time. Why does that happen? Because motivation that leads to consistent action comes primarily from within. We have to keep focused on our goals. And we have to develop the habit of tackling the tasks necessary to achieve those goals. The goal may be years away, but the satisfaction that comes from doing what needs to be done is a daily reward.

CHAPTER 13

MANAGE YOUR COLLEGE CAREER

In high school, perhaps your Mom woke you up in the morning and urged you to hurry and get ready. While you took a shower, Mom prepared your favorite breakfast. As you inhaled her cooking, she reassured you that you were ready to do well on the math test—after all, she had reminded you to study the night before. Mom put an overstuffed lunch bag in your hand as you rushed out the door.

The summer after high school flashes by...suddenly you're in college. Your alarm goes off at 7AM, just in time to shower, dress, have breakfast, and make your 8AM history class. But you were up late last night, and you've discovered the wonders of the snooze button (a feature moms don't have). You hit snooze once, twice.... You think, "I just won't take a shower, won't eat, won't look over my notes one last time." Then, a truly big thought: "If I blow off this class I could sleep for another two hours—my next class isn't until 10AM." Mom would call and make you get up if she knew what was going on. But this is college. It's about freedom and trust. Your roommate is not a great source of inspiration. He's sleeping off a hangover, but he doesn't have to worry. His parents donated a wing to the school library.

Yes, college is a great opportunity. But where there is opportunity there is also danger. If you've prepared well in high school, you're ready to take advantage of everything college has to offer. But if you think college will be easy—or if you just don't think about it—you're setting yourself up for an upset. College demands far more than high school. You will do well if you assume it will be hard and bear down from day one. It's imperative that you get off to a good start and stay on top of your studies. If you get behind, it's hard to catch up. You feel overwhelmed and stressed out, and it becomes hard to have a good time even when you are playing your sport or relaxing with your friends.

Selecting a major

Every college student has to decide what to specialize in. So you might major in History, Computer Science, Biology, Physical Education, Business, English, or any of dozens of other subjects. Particularly in your final two or three years in college, you'll probably take several courses in your major in each semester.

Some athletic programs steer you toward easy majors or even majors specially devised for athletes. "Majoring in eligibility" means you might end up with a college degree that represents little learning and is useless toward getting a job.

Select a major based on what you want to learn, what career you're interested in, or both. Keep in mind that some majors may conflict with your sport more than others. For example, let's say you want to be a doctor. A pre-med major requires taking many laboratory courses in chemistry and biology. The lab hours may overlap your practice times. To pursue your sport and be a pre-med student would take careful planning. You might have to take some lab courses during the off season, during the summer, or after you had used up your athletic eligibility.

When you start college you have a year or two to decide on a major. Use your experience in selecting a college to help you. Investigate. Take elective courses in areas of study you are considering. Ask professors in the department about their courses, graduate school and/or jobs in the field, and whatever else you need to know to choose wisely.

Time management in college

Your sport, including practice, physical therapy, weight training, watching films, team meetings, travel, and games, may take up 40 hours a week. The NCAA restricts your coach to requiring no more than 20 hours a week, with additional time on a voluntary basis. "Volunteers" tend to get the playing time.

If you are taking a full schedule of courses, you will be in class 15 hours a week. There are 168 hours in a week. After classes, sports, and the time necessary for a good night's sleep and three meals a day, you're left with about six hours a day to brush your teeth, do the laundry, clean your room, socialize—and study.

You can do this if you manage your time efficiently, which we talked about in Chapter 7. The time you put into your sport is structured by the coach. Studying has to be worked in around that. You finish a long, hard practice. You take a quick shower, grab a bite, and then you have to make a decision. Do I shut my eyes for a short nap, maybe catch a *Beavis and Butt-Head* rerun, or do I get my butt into the library for three hours of study?

Plan to plan

In college, where there is less structure than in high school and no one is holding your hand, planning is more critical than ever. To manage your time efficiently takes time, but a little bit goes a long way. You might decide that every Sunday at 8PM you're going to spend 30 minutes planning your week, and also looking ahead to the following weeks and months. And that every morning you're going to spend five minutes reviewing the plan for that day and making any necessary changes. For most people, a plan is not a plan until it is written down.

The basics of time management are simple. Focus on what's important and/or urgent. If math is your biggest problem, make sure you schedule enough time to study math. If you're applying for summer jobs and the applications have to go out next week, schedule time to work on your resumé right away.

If you don't schedule your time, you could work hard, but fail. You could spend your time working on the wrong things. If you're getting good grades in Spanish, English, and history, but failing math, chances are you're not budgeting your time correctly.

Make commitments to yourself and others

We all tend to do things we're good at and that we enjoy, and to put off the tough stuff, those "boring" things that we "hate." Your plan says study, but you'd rather go out with your friends, watch TV, play a video game, sleep. Anything but take care of the real business at hand. Once you've made your plan, be committed to carrying it out. Refuse to be diverted. Your plan to study math at 8PM is a promise to yourself. If you're tired, or if your friends are watching TV, your resolve may weaken. That's when you ask yourself, "Am I going to break this promise?"

Sometimes it's easier to keep a promise when other people are involved. Suppose you arrange to meet a friend at the library after dinner to study math. You are more likely to do it, even if you're tired.

To transfer or not to transfer

Hopefully you picked a school and an athletic program that are right for you, and nothing is interfering with your enjoyment of your college experience.

What if you made a mistake in selecting a college or if things have changed—either with the college or with you—since you arrived? What if you are no longer enjoying your sport?

Think the problem through; talk about it with coaches, advisors, parents, friends. Do everything you can to find a solution within the program. Transferring to another school is not an automatic ticket to happiness. You may find that the school you switch to is worse! If you are a Division I hockey player or basketball player (male or female) or a Division IA football player, NCAA rules require sitting out a year after you transfer. Some athletic conferences require sitting out two years if you transfer to another college within the conference. College academic departments often don't accept all the credits students have earned elsewhere, which can delay graduation.

If your problem cannot be solved within your program, you've either got to live with it or make a move. In NCAA Division I or II, you must be released from your athletic scholarship to transfer and play elsewhere. Colleges are more frequently refusing to release athletes. Their position is that they have made a commitment to scholarship athletes and that it's not fair to the program for athletes to be free to leave on a whim.

This logic has holes in it. Athletic scholarships are renewable one year at a time, so a college's commitment has an element of "What have you done for us lately?" And coaches can leave anytime, no matter how many years are left on their contracts.

Your college may say that even if you don't like their food, you've got to stay and eat as long as they are putting it on the table. If you are determined to leave, however, they have to let you go. Slavery was abolished in this country over 120 years ago, even if some of the NCAA rules appear to bring it back. Sometimes the college uses its refusal to release you as a bargaining chip: "We'll let you go if you don't go to another school in the conference, or if you don't follow an assistant to the school where he is now head coach." Fortunately, most coaches understand that it's not in their best interest to stand in the way of an athlete who wants to leave.

CHAPTER 14

CHALLENGES FACING COLLEGE ATHLETES

Swelled heads (and self doubt)

A TV talk show host asked a star actor, whose husband is also a movie star, what their child thought about having two famous parents. "She's not impressed," the actor said, "she thinks everybody's parents are on TV."

Maybe you were a star on your high school team. You were sought after by hundreds of students who didn't even know if they liked you. They just wanted some of your glory to reflect on them. Teachers and administrators went out of their way to make things easy for you. Like the movie star's child, you may not even have realized you were receiving special treatment.

At college you may continue to get star treatment. Or suddenly you may be spending a lot of time on the bench. Either way, some students and professors will think you haven't got the brains to be at their school.

Don't rate yourself by what others think. You're who you are, whether others are foolish enough to worship you or sneer at you. Try to be objective about your abilities, athletic or academic, and work on improving them.

More things in heaven and earth than ESPN and Nike

You spend hours every day with your teammates. You travel together, and share an interest in the same sport. Naturally, you become close friends with some of them.

It may not be as easy to make friends with people who don't play organized sports, especially if you live in a dorm exclusively for athletes. The extra effort is well worth it. Spend time with people who do not share your experiences and assumptions and you will have one of the finest educational opportunities college has to offer: learning how others view the world. There's a famous line from *Hamlet*: "There are more things in heaven and earth, Horatio, than are dreamt of in your philosophy." You don't need *Cliffs Notes* to know Shakespeare got that one right. Today, more than ever, there is so much going on, and each of us is exposed to only a small part of it. In college you can meet people who grew up in New York City or Ulan Bator, people who can open your mind to everything from astrophysics to zoology.

You will value your friendships with fellow athletes for a lifetime, but don't limit your circle to athletes, or to people of the same race, religion, nationality, or background as yourself. Hate and prejudice are passed down through generations of people who never bother to see things from the perspective of others. On TV, complex historical, religious, and cultural questions are reduced to sound bytes, often of angry people trying to drown each other out. College students have the opportunity to sit down and talk with people of different views, and to learn from each other. You can draw on other cultures and areas of knowledge and incorporate aspects of them into your own life. Broadening your outlook will help you succeed in today's global society.

The world on your shoulders

If you're in a big-time college program that's getting media coverage, the emotional ups and downs of athletic competition can reach another level of intensity. Commentators and writers will describe games as though the fate of civilization depended on their outcome. Boosters and fans will express themselves with similar hyperbole. You might find your coach, your teammates, or yourself glorified or denounced on TV, radio, or in print.

When the pressure is on, it's more important than ever to stay on an even keel and retain your sense of humor and your sense of proportion.

Gambling: "a tax on imbeciles"

Gambling is a huge problem in our society. It can be every bit as addicting as alcohol or drugs. Sure, in moderation, gambling can be controlled. After all, much of it is legal. You wager a couple bucks on a game of pool or the state lottery, or make a friendly bet on the big game. But, if you're a competitive person (and what athlete isn't?), once you start down this path, it can be hard to stop. A couple of dollars wagered on a game of H-O-R-S-E can escalate to betting $50 on your favorite team. If you lose, we hope you realize when it's time to stop. Unfortunately, athletes tend to believe they'll win the next time out. In sports, this can be a great trait. It can motivate you to learn more each time about what it takes to win, and to prepare better. In gambling, it's a formula for disaster because lost bets do not provide any clues.

An epidemic of gambling on sports is sweeping college campuses, involving athletes and non-athletes alike. Many students go way beyond an occasional recreational bet. They become addicted. They squander their tuition money, their food money, their rent money, and go deeply into debt. As they lose, they keep believing that they are going to come out ahead, make something for nothing, beat the system. They haven't quite figured out where the money comes from to build all those big hotel casinos in Las Vegas and Atlantic City. Someone defined gambling as "a tax on imbeciles."

Rules against gambling

The NCAA prohibits college athletes from gambling on any sport. This means that a water polo player violates NCAA rules if he places a bet on a professional basketball game. If you are caught gambling on sports, the punishment is usually severe, up to permanent ineligibility. Gambling on sports is usually treated more harshly than being caught with illegal drugs, for example. It makes no difference to the NCAA if the bet is made illegally through a bookie or legally through a Las Vegas sports book. If you go to Vegas and lose your shirt on the slot machines or at the crap table, that is not a violation of NCAA rules, although it is certainly a rotten idea. But gambling on sports is absolutely prohibited.

The logic behind the NCAA's position is that college athletes and gambling on sports must be kept as far apart as possible, to avoid any appearance that games might be fixed. Gambling on professional and college sports is a billion-dollar industry. In the real world, football and basketball are usually the only college sports on which there is widespread gambling, legal and illegal.

Point shaving

Especially in football and basketball, gamblers (often with ties to organized crime) may try to get you to fix a game, by "shaving points" for example. Or they may seek information from you about how prepared the team is or whether a teammate has recovered from an injury or illness. The best strategy: don't provide anybody with information that is not available to the general public.

Fixing games is not just a violation of NCAA rules. It is a federal crime. You can go to jail. In fact, if you are offered money by a gambler and you don't take it, but you don't report it, that is a violation of the law and of NCAA rules. If you are approached by a gambler, immediately go to your coach with the facts—even if other players are involved. Loyalty is a great quality, but people involved in criminal activities do not deserve your loyalty. The best tip we can give you is don't gamble.

Agents of corruption

If you show the potential for professional football, basketball, baseball, hockey, tennis, golf, or track and field, sports agents may start trying to develop relationships with you while you're still in college (or even high school). Getting caught signing a contract with an agent disqualifies you from competing in college.

YOU BET YOUR LIFE

Taking money or anything else directly or indirectly from an agent is also a violation of NCAA, NAIA, and NJCAA rules. If caught, you will be suspended or disqualified.

Agents compete to represent the few who make it to the pros. The prizes are big: percentages of multimillion dollar salaries and endorsement contracts. It's hard to know who will make it, so agents try to develop ties with as many pro prospects as possible. Less scrupulous agents try to buy your friendship with parties, cars, cash, hotel rooms, air fares—whatever will work.

College coaches want to keep agents away from college players. They have conflicting interests. Some agents, especially desperate ones with few clients, want athletes to jump to the pros as soon as possible, so they can start taking their cut. Coaches generally want the best athletes to stay in college, to keep the games exciting and the TV ratings high. And of course so the athletes can get their degrees.

Even if you don't get caught, you will be in debt to an agent you've taken favors from. If you make it to the pros, you'll feel obliged to select that agent. Wouldn't you rather be represented by an agent who spends time doing deals and negotiating contracts for the people he or she represents than by a sleazeball who gave you money and stroked your ego?

The bottom line for dealing with sports agents

There is nothing wrong with talking to an agent. There are good agents out there, as well as plenty of bad apples. Do not believe you can tell them apart just by talking. When the time comes to select an agent, you will have to go through a careful process, just as you did in selecting a college. Meanwhile, as difficult as it may be if you don't have two nickels to rub together, don't take anything from an agent. It may eat you up inside that everyone around you is getting rich off your talents, and you have little or nothing to show for it (especially if you're not going to class). But no agent can give you enough to risk your college athletic career.

When NBA player Marcus Camby was at UMass, he took money, clothes, cars, and stereos from two unscrupulous agents.

Not only Camby, but also his family and friends. When Camby didn't sign with either agent, they threatened to expose him and to break his bones. Camby escaped physical damage, but ended up reimbursing the agents. The NCAA stripped UMass from the 1996 Final Four record book and required the school to return $151,000. Camby repaid that sum as well.

Some agents use associates, known as "bird dogs," to get close to athletes. Bird dogs don't always say they represent agents. They may just start hanging around and befriending you. If you accept a gift, and it comes out that the gift giver is associated with an agent, you pay the penalty, not the agent or the bird dog. Bottom line: There is no Santa Claus coming down the locker room chimney. Agents give gifts to get something in return.

Boosters: the ups and downs

Supporters of the team may also offer you gifts. It's a violation of NCAA rules to accept gifts from boosters. Basically, you are not allowed to receive any financial reward for playing your sport other than an athletic scholarship.

If you haven't got much money and suddenly you find yourselves among students who drive fancy cars and dress like they're from *90210*, it's hard to say no to gifts. It seems unfair, especially if you're on a team that brings millions of dollars into the school. Still, you're better off not taking from the boosters. You put yourself in a position where you could be suspended or disqualified—a big risk to take for a suit, an airplane ticket, or even a car.

There is something far more valuable than gifts that you can legally and ethically accept from boosters. Boosters tend to be prominent business and professional people. They can give you information and advice in their areas of expertise, and leads to summer jobs and to employment after you graduate. A booster might even be able to give you a summer job in his or her own business. Sometimes a booster will offer you a cushy job that is basically just a pretext to give you money. You're better off with a real job where you can learn something that will help you after you graduate. Boosters may also be willing to provide you with personal references and letters of recommendation for graduate schools and jobs, and introductions to other people who can help you.

Conflicts with coaches

If you understand each other from the beginning, you can develop a great relationship with your coach and never have a significant problem.

Sometimes, though, things don't work out as expected. It's best to be prepared for conflicts, so that if one does arise, you can handle it intelligently.

Coach says, "Be a team player"

That's generally good advice. A bunch of athletes going after individual glory is a formula for failure. But what if the coach wants you to take easy courses that conflict with your educational goals? Or if the coach wants you to play in an important game despite an injury and you think it might be a bad medical risk? The coach may talk about loyalty and sacrifice for the team. Loyalty is a two-way street. Has the coach sacrificed any part of his or her agenda out of loyalty to you? These situations can be complicated; there are no pat answers. Sometimes it's right to make sacrifices for the team; sometimes your first loyalty must be to yourself. Use your judgment and seek advice from people you trust.

Don't cheat yourself out of an education

If you are having problems staying eligible and the team needs you, someone may offer to write a history paper or take a French test for you. Everyone knows this happens, because athletes and non-athletes get caught every day.

Can a school have a championship athletic program without compromising its academic mission? Yes. But only if everyone from the college president to the athletic director to the professors to the coaching staff to the tutors to the boosters are committed to playing by the rules. Everyone that's involved with the athletic department must strike a healthy balance between the desire to have a winning sports program and the necessity to provide the best possible academic environment.

So what should you do if you're behind in your schoolwork and someone offers to cheat for you? It's tempting to accept such "help." It solves your immediate problems and for every athlete who gets caught, probably dozens or even hundreds don't.

Why not take a chance if the odds are good?

Because all students who cheat (including the many non-athletes who do so) get caught. They get caught short. Twice, in fact.

First, they don't learn the material necessary to prepare them for more advanced courses, for graduate school, for a career, and for becoming knowledgeable adults. Cheating leads to more cheating, as when you tell a lie, and have to tell another lie to cover up the first one.

Second, cheaters learn to look for the easy way out of difficult situations. The easy way out often leads to failed marriages, addiction, broken careers, even jail. What looks easy can end up being very hard indeed. Shortcuts may not take you where you want to go.

Help is available

Most colleges offer tutoring. If you're having trouble with a course, students who have mastered that subject can help you. Often, there are extra resources available especially for athletes: tutors, academic advisors, counselors.

If you need help, get it. Take advantage of the programs that are available. Don't wait until you're failing. Seek help as soon as you realize there's a problem that you can't solve by yourself.

Beware. There is a point at which tutoring crosses the line between helping you learn and doing the work for you. It's tempting to go along, even if neither you nor the tutor set out to cheat. But you'd be cheating yourself. Make it clear to the tutor that you want to learn. If necessary, go to the person in charge of the tutoring program and make sure you are assigned a tutor who will help you understand the material, but will not do the work for you.

Academic requirements
for staying eligible

Athletic governing bodies require athletes to be "full-time students" and to make progress toward a degree to remain eligible. The NCAA, NAIA, and NJCAA define "full-time student" as one who takes a minimum of 12 credits per semester. The NCAA also requires Division I athletes to comply with the 25-50-75 rule. This rule says that by the end of your second year, you have to have completed 25% of the requirements for graduation; by the end of your third year, 50%; and by the end of your fourth year, 75%. Requirements for graduation refers to all academic requirements, not just total number of credits. For example, if you're a History major and the Department requires that you take twelve History courses to graduate, you will need to take nine of those courses (75%) by the end of your fourth year.

The 25-50-75 rule recognizes that with the additional demands of your sport, it can take you five rather than four years to go through college. You are only required to complete one quarter of your academic work in the first two years, so the rule allows you to adjust to college and take remedial courses if you need them. But it does require you to look ahead, beginning with your freshman year, and make a 5-year plan that keeps you eligible and does not give you some semesters that are too easy in exchange for other semesters with impossible academic loads.

Coaches and athletic departments want to keep you eligible, but they have different outlooks on how to do it. Some programs are seriously interested in helping you learn. Others just want you to stay eligible on paper for as long as possible. They steer you toward easy courses, some of which may be especially created to keep athletes eligible. Going along with such schemes is just another way to cheat yourself out of a college education. Remember that the courses you take and the major you choose are ultimately up to you. Take the most challenging courses you are capable of. Don't base such important decisions on what's easy in the short run.

CHAPTER 15

JUMPING TO THE PROS (SKIP THIS CHAPTER)

This chapter is about going pro before completing four years of college. You probably shouldn't read it. As you know, few athletes go on to earn a living from their sport. However, a disturbing trend has emerged. Many athletes are making a beeline to the professional ranks even though most are clearly not ready. It's probably not going to change, the money's too huge. But if an athlete takes a long, objective look at this decision, it might make better sense to stay in college (or go to college!) even when a lucrative pro contract is on the table.

A young person becomes rich and famous, financially set, free from the demands of the everyday world. The story gets huge media coverage, because it appeals to our imaginations, and because it's so exceptional. We hear about the 17-year-old who is a top NBA pick straight out of high school, and signs national endorsement contracts before playing his first pro game. We hear about the running back who jumps to the NFL after his third year, is selected in the first round of the draft, and goes on to a Hall of Fame career.

But we hear little or nothing about more typical cases, such as the quarterback who went pro after his junior year, based on an agent's estimate that he'd be a first-round pick. At the scouting combine, it was discovered that the QB was smaller and slower than he was thought to be, and his skills not quite as sharp. He wasn't taken until the seventh round of the draft, and he signed for a salary close to the league minimum. Unless you regularly monitor the microscopic "Transactions" in the Sports Section, you probably wouldn't know that he was let go after his rookie year. Leaving college early is a big media deal, but getting cut is strictly back-page material. This is too bad, because the mistakes of others can be great lessons for us. If we know about them.

Get there and stay

Many athletes are so focused on getting into professional sports that they never think beyond that. The goal isn't to get to the pros, it's to stay in the pros. Do you want to be a first-round pick, sign a rookie contract, and then be out of the League after a couple of seasons? Or is your goal to have a 10-year career?

College prepares you for a job, whether in business, medicine, law, or sports. It is the place to hone the skills you need to succeed in your chosen profession. Playing three or four years of ACC or Pac-10 basketball, for example, is great training, even if your alternative is to be a lottery pick straight out of high school or after a year of college.

The NBA is picking players—Kevin Garnett, Kobe Bryant, Tracey McGrady, Jermaine O'Neal, Rashard Lewis—not because of how great they were in high school, but because of their enormous potential. Often, potential is based more on hype than objective evaluation. Most of these players have struggled at the NBA level. The same goes for many athletes who left college after one or two years. College graduates Grant Hill, Keith Van Horn, and Tim Duncan were a different story. They showed up Day One prepared for the rigors of the NBA. The rule of thumb used to be you needed to stay in school at least three years. Bottom line: college was good enough for Michael Jordan for three years.

You may decide that you want to stay in college no matter how many millions pro sports may offer. The reasons could include

- getting a degree
- satisfying your parents
- enjoyment of college sports

- a goal such as a championship or individual award
- improving your athletic skills
- mental and physical conditioning
- maturing emotionally

Cash in now...or later?

Your Uncle Larry gives you a gift: 100,000 shares of stock in Mercury Shoes. You could sell it now at $1 per share. This is tempting, because you've got $7.57 in your pocket, and you think $100,000 could be the ticket to your dreams.

Mercury is a new company that has developed a revolutionary basketball shoe. Uncle Larry gave you a pair, and they are phenomenal. Most people have never heard of Merx, but almost everyone who tries them says they are the best basketball shoe ever made. The company has production problems, and needs to develop a distribution network. To become well known, Mercury plans to sign the NBA's next Michael Jordan.

If you sell the stock now, your big decision will be whether to go to the car dealer first or to the mall. But Uncle Larry keeps saying Mercury could be the next Microsoft. You think, "How will I feel if I sell this stock for $1 a share, and three or four years from now it's at $10, or $20, or $30, or…?"

Then you think, "But there's always the chance the company will fold. Then I wouldn't even get my $100,000. And I sure could use a new car…."

Now think of yourself as a stock. The decision to stay in school or go pro is similar to the one about selling stock now or later. Instant wealth is tempting, particularly if you've never had much money. Who wouldn't want to buy his mom a nice house, and pull up to visit her in a luxury car? But who wants to look back and realize that by waiting a year or two, he could have done far better? Especially when a year or two seems much shorter when you're looking back.

Go pro, young man (or woman)

What rare combination of circumstances might make it reasonable to turn pro before finishing college?

- an objective estimate of your value as a pro
- a high level of athletic development
- the maturity to cope with life in the pros

Take a closer look at each of these points.

An objective estimate of your value as a pro

If you are going to be a top five pick in most professional leagues, you will sign a contract that will guarantee you millions of dollars. Let's face it, unless you are committed to staying in college for the reasons mentioned earlier, that much money is hard to pass up.

You don't know with any degree of certainty where you'll be picked in the draft. This is a big problem. In football, once you declare yourself eligible for the draft, there is no going back, even if you end up not being drafted at all, or if you are drafted but get cut. In basketball, there can be a reprieve. You can go pro, and return either before the draft or if you go undrafted. If you expected to be a top pick, but drop to last, you're stuck.

It's hard for young athletes to analyze where they will go in the draft. Even general managers, who are paid to predict how well athletes will perform as pros, make embarrassing mistakes. The athlete's problem is complicated by ego, media hype, the hopes and wishes of family and friends, and by advice from people with a financial stake in the decision. For example, an agent may imply that a high level inside source with a team has told him they will "definitely select you" with their eighth pick in the first round. Now the athlete thinks he can do no worse than eighth, and could go higher.

Anyone who makes such a statement is a liar. No GM commits to a player before making a full evaluation at all-star games, scouting combines, and individual testing. That process doesn't start for an underclassman until he applies for the draft. With the exception of athletes who are clearly the cream of the crop, all you can really get is a reasonable estimate as to where you are projected to be drafted. Unfortunately, that's not much reassurance when such a major decision is involved. A player thought to be a fourth round pick can move himself up to a first round pick in a

© 1999 AthleteNetwork.com

short time. Just as quickly, a "sure-fire first round pick" can plummet right out of the draft. The reality is that even on draft day teams often don't know who they're going to take. There are just too many variables.

If you play an individual sport such as golf or tennis there is no draft and no contract. You become a pro by qualifying and entering pro competitions. Your earnings are based on how high you place in those competitions. Just as for a team sport player, it comes down to analyzing your abilities. There's no denying Tiger Woods made the right decision in leaving Stanford after his Sophomore year. But there are plenty of names which escape us (and everyone else) who did the same thing with different results.

Turning pro before your eligibility expires is always a gamble. How can an athlete make the most objective estimate? By using the same techniques that work in the college recruiting process:

- ask questions
- listen
- don't rely on the advice of only one person
- understand the financial interests of everyone involved
- take time to think and rethink, don't decide under pressure
- check that your decision conforms to your basic values

High level of athletic development

As anyone who has worked at minimum wage knows, an employer pays you to perform. Make a mistake at $5.00 an hour and you might be calmly taught how to do it right. At $3,000,000 per year, employers tend to be more impatient about getting results. The pros may draft you high because of your potential, but they sure aren't going to wait patiently for you to live up to it. With that kind of money at stake, they want to see it now. If your skills or body need more time to develop, staying in college will increase your chances of succeeding in the pros. Working with your college coach for another year or two can make a significant difference. Think it through. Focus on making yourself the best athlete you can become. The money will follow.

Maturity to cope with life in the pros

Professional sports is much tougher than even big-time college sports (and in a different universe from high school sports). Everything becomes magnified: the media, the fans, and talk radio view professional sports as fair game. It comes with the territory, along with money, cars, houses, and all that the good life has to offer. If your game falls slightly below the unreasonable expectations, you become an easy target for brutal criticism. Understand how rigorous this can be and ask yourself if you're ready. Life in the pros is not revealed on television. It has nothing to do with what we see on *Inside Stuff*. (No offense, Ahmad.) The "NBA is fantastic"—for the fans. And it is glamorous to play in the NBA. But it's also a grind: the grueling schedule, the intense pain, the travel, the hotels, the media, the fans. Other professional sports are equally demanding. You might decide another year or two of emotional and intellectual maturity would help you succeed as a pro even if, as an athlete, you are ready now.

Going pro for the wrong reasons

Academic ineligibility

If you turn pro mainly because you're faced with losing your eligibility, you allow yourself to be controlled by events rather than controlling them. Knee-jerk decisions based on choosing the lesser of two evils usually lead to disaster. There is a better solution. Sit out a year and focus on academics. At the same time work on parts of your game that need development. You can end up a better student and a better athlete, a person with the toughness of mind to deal with life in pro sports or in another career.

Deciding to stay in school under these circumstances takes patience: sitting out a season can seem like the end of the world. But going pro because you are forced into it is a truly risky proposition. There is a good chance you will overestimate your chances in the draft because you feel you have no choice. There's another problem. If you are not eligible because you've never taken academics seriously, you may have little knowledge of anything outside your sport. This could make you a prime candidate for getting misled or ripped off by unscrupulous agents, business managers, and assorted con-men and hangers-on. Screwing up your eligibility should be an alarm telling you to get your priorities straight.

Fear of injury

An athlete who could make hundreds of thousands or even millions in a season certainly doesn't want to lose that income if he or she is injured while playing for free. The risk is small, however, compared to the risks of going pro before you are ready. And there is a way to hedge your bet. College athletes are permitted by the NCAA to purchase disability insurance which pays as much as $3 million in case of a career-ending injury. The NCAA even has a program to help pro-caliber athletes get loans to pay the insurance premiums.

To go or not to go?

That is the question trying the souls of many athletes. Get the best advice you can get. Then, it's your responsibility to evaluate the advice, make a decision, and live with it, just as when you selected a college. Career choice is not an exact science. You will never know if you made the right decision except in hindsight and maybe not even then. You may be the rare exception that can thrive in the pros at a young age. We do know that for every success story, many athletes leave school only to see their dreams of pro glory become nightmares. Pro sports isn't going anywhere. It will be around a year from now. And so will the money (probably in greater amounts). Our overall advice: If in doubt, wait it out.

Warning to those who should have skipped this chapter

We've been talking to the small number of athletes who are legitimate pro prospects. For each one of them, there are thousands of young athletes who get caught up in the hoopla. They dream about playing on national television and driving a BMW when they should be studying algebra.

CHAPTER 16

PREPARING FOR
LIFE AFTER COLLEGE

Life after college is the payoff for all the work you've been doing, from day one in high school and before. Every word in this book has been written to help make your time in the "real world" rewarding. Not that it's ever going to be a piece of cake, but by now you don't expect that. College was tougher than high school; the exams you will have to pass in your profession and as a spouse and parent will be even more challenging.

The key to success in college was early preparation in high school. For example, starting in the ninth grade you looked ahead to see what you had to do to be admitted to the college of your choice. You also found out what you needed to do to be eligible to compete in your sport once you got there.

Similarly, early preparation in college is the key to success after graduation. If you're thinking about getting an advanced degree, what courses do you have to take to be eligible for graduate schools in your field? What entrance exams must you prepare for? If you intend to get a job immediately after college, what majors are employers in your field looking for? Are there summer jobs or internships that will help you be the most qualified candidate?

Clearly, the time to start thinking about these issues is in your freshman year, while there is still plenty of time to act on your decisions. "Are you crazy?" asked one stressed-out freshman. "It's hard enough just to go to practice everyday and keep up with my courses. I don't have time to dry off after I shower, let alone think about stuff four years down the road."

That's one way to look at it. Another point of view is that an eye on the future will keep you motivated and help you decide which immediate demands are most important and which are a waste of time.

I don't know what to do with the rest of my life

Some students arrive at college with a precise career goal. "I'm going to be a brain surgeon; a systems analyst; an entrepreneur; a patent attorney."

You may not be one of these tightly focused whiz kids. Don't worry, you are in the clueless majority. And even students who have traveled for a year after graduating, or hung out at their parents' homes until they were kicked out, have gone on to accomplish great things. We suggest that you view your uncertainty as an opportunity rather than a problem. College is the perfect place to explore the hundreds of career possibilities. Talk to other students—especially juniors and seniors—about what their plans are and why they chose them. Take elective courses to find out if a field interests you and if you have an aptitude for it. In fact, even if you have been certain since age six that you were going to be an electrical engineer (after breaking Jackie Joyner-Kersee's world record in the heptathlon), college is a great time to step back, ask yourself why, and investigate alternatives. Statistics tell us you are likely to change careers at least once during your lifetime. Don't be afraid to try new things during and after college to find out if they are for you. Even if you decide they're not, the experience will be useful in whatever you do.

Career center

Your college is almost certain to have a career center, or some similarly named entity that helps students prepare for life after college. Become familiar with this place as soon as you can. The center may have a library of information about exciting and rewarding careers you never heard of or were only dimly aware of. Technology and life are changing so fast that new fields constantly emerge. The 70s and 80s saw the advent of environmental law, sports medicine, sports psychology, and personal trainers, to mention just a few. The 90s has seen the Internet become a major factor in commerce and life, and the explosion of Internet-related careers. Executive coaching has also become a growing phenomenon. Business people and professionals have discovered what athletes have always known, that a good coach can be vital to success.

Investigate all the resources available in the career center. In addition to information about careers, they may include

Career assessment This involves tests to help determine what fields fit your values, skills, experience, interests, personality, and goals. For example, you probably won't want a career in software engineering if constant tracking of thousands of details isn't your thing. Knowing what you want from a job and what you have to offer prospective employers will be a strategic advantage in your job search. What are your priorities? Job fulfillment? Money? Experience? Opportunity to travel?

Resume preparation Your resume is a key self-marketing tool, designed to obtain a job interview. It should market your skills, knowledge, and accomplishments relevant to the career field and even the specific potential employer. If you have the opportunity to read sample resumes and cover letters, and to get help from experts who have written hundreds of them, take advantage of it.

Mock job interviews An interview can be one of the big games of your life. Yet many people go in with no practice. Your career center may offer to videotape your mock interview and review and critique it with you. You'll want to be prepared to answer questions about your qualifications and goals thoroughly and honestly. You should know how to deal with tough questions, and of course how to present yourself in the most favorable possible light.

Even more important than the technical resources of the career center are the people who work there. Get to know them. They can give you inside information about trends in the job market. They talk to recruiters (read: people offering jobs with paychecks) every day. Just imagine how nice it would be if, during these conversations, your career goals were on their minds and your name at the tip of their tongues.

Online job services for students

There are two Web sites that can be of great help to your job search, whether you get to them through your career center or on your own.

StudentCenter.com

StudentCenter.com helps demystify the job-search process by emphasizing the importance of research and preparation. StudentCenter.com can help you identify your personal strengths, define their career goals, and fine tune your resume writing and interview skills.

JobTrak.com

JobTrak.com is an electronic meat market (in the best possible sense, of course). It brings employers together with job seekers. In the old days (we're talking one year ago), you would place your resume on file in the career center. Recruiters would dig through piles of paper resumes to find candidates. Now everything's done online. Many schools use the JobTrak.com service exclusively. You post your resume electronically so that recruiters can find it in the database.

Getting your first job

If you were heavily recruited by college coaches, seeking your first job can be an eye-opener. Even if you have solid credentials such as good grades and strong extra-curricular activities, you may be competing against many other well qualified candidates. In sports, your skills are relatively easy to showcase. In seeking a job, you're judged more on things like speaking ability and writing skills. Remember, though, a lot of the same qualities that made you successful in sports lead to success in the business world. Communicate those abilities. Let them know you're a leader and a team player. That you can take direction. That you can think on your feet. That you can take initiative to start and finish projects. Package yourself to prospective employers so that they can see that you are prepared for your career.

Additional tips for landing a job

Especially if you are seeking a general, non-career-related position, you may be asked to complete and return a formal application. Be sure to fill out these forms neatly and thoroughly, typing them when possible. Immediately after an interview, always send a thank-you letter to the interviewer expressing your appreciation. Be sure to get the interviewer's name and title and the company name and address right. The best way is to ask the interviewer for his or her business card. Paying attention to these details will often separate you from the pack. You would think that nobody would ever be foolish enough to misspell the name of an interviewer or the name of a company, but it happens frequently. Then again, why should it be any different from sports, where many athletes make the same fundamental errors over and over again?

Anything you can do to acquire real world experience makes you more valuable to an employer, and therefore more marketable. If your schedule permits, seek an internship during the summer or academic year. Exposure to your chosen field may help you discover you'd really rather do something else—or that you like it even more than you expected. Boosters may be able to help you get experience in your field, through their own businesses or those of their friends and associates. Parents of teammates and other friends might be able to provide similar help. Don't hesitate to ask.

If you arrive at college without good typing and other computer-related skills, acquiring them while at college is a must. Computer literacy, including the ability to use the Internet, are fundamental in virtually every area of work today.

Keeping a job and moving up

Getting hired is only another beginning, like making the team. To thrive in the competitive job market, you need to learn how to become ever more valuable to your employer, associates, and clients. Just as playing time is determined by your coach based on your performance, your boss will make decisions which impact your job responsibilities, opportunities, and salary.

Be proactive about your career. Many workers are content to sit back, thinking any new job skills they need will be taught to them by the company at the appropriate time. In the past, that may have been true. But lifetime employment with one company has become a rarity. In the incredibly competitive global economy, employers look to trim expenses whenever possible. When the time comes for the ax to fall, it will be too late for you to prove you're vital to the company's performance. According to a study by the National Research Council, it now takes only three to five years for 50 percent of the average worker's skills to become obsolete. To make yourself valuable to a present or future employer requires that you work constantly on improving your skills. This concept should come as no shock to an athlete: it's what coaches have been telling you since day one. Don't rely only on your good looks and sweet personality to stay employed. Be an expert in your job and know other people's as well, like a utility player on a baseball team. In a business world that measures results, competence is a treasured commodity.

The idea of an "employer," particularly after you've gained some experience in your business or profession, is no longer the only norm. Many tasks today are accomplished by loose strategic alliances of professionals in a variety of disciplines, who break up after the project is completed and reform for the next one. Even recent college graduates work as freelancers and start their own business.

Networking

As a college athlete, you are likely to be invited to functions at school and in the community: luncheons, banquets, award presentations, founding ceremonies, anniversaries of organizations, and so on. Athletes tend to look on these occasions as a burden. Focus on your future and you will see these affairs as opportunities rather than obligations. You're in a relaxed environment with successful business and professional people with whom you share a common interest. Rather than just sit with other athletes, approach these people and talk to them. Take an interest in what they do. (Even astonish your friends by talking to their parents.) They will be delighted to get to know you, and they can be of great help to you after college. The "old boy network" is a terrible thing—until you (male or female) benefit from it. The reality is that job opportunities are based on merit *and* who you know. Preparing yourself to be good in your field and developing a strong list of contacts is a powerful combination for success.

Networking after college

Virtually every field has one or more professional or trade associations. It's never too soon to research these organizations and join and become active in the appropriate ones. You can learn a great deal that will help make you more knowledgeable and effective in your work, and you can make invaluable contacts.

In today's quickly-changing workplace, you are unlikely to be doing the same thing over and over again for years. You are likely to receive many short-term assignments. Through these assignments you will meet a wide range of people at many levels in and outside your organization. Take advantage of these opportunities to get to know these people and weave them into your web of contacts. They and their associates may be in a position to help your career at some point in your future.

The Real Athletes Credo on page 7 counsels against settling for the minimum, on or off the field. This certainly applies to business and the professions. You may have an opportunity to pitch in and help your associates finish a project on time, even if it isn't your responsibility to do so. It might require sacrifices, such as skipping lunch, staying late or even take some work home. But going the extra yard can demonstrate your abilities and drive, and create a situation where people will want to help you.

Networking is a 2-way street

The single best way to gain from networking is by helping the people in your network. The more you help them, the more they will want to help you, rather than view you as a pushy person who is always asking for favors. And when you help one person, others find out about it and join in appreciating what you did. Pay attention to people's needs and wants, and see where you can be of help. Early in your career, you may feel limited in what you can do. But it's amazing what happens when you put your mind to helping others. Suddenly you remember, for example, that your cousin Henry's company has a need for exactly the services that Jill, a person in your network, provides.

Have a mentor

"Mentor" is a buzzword for a friend who is more experienced than you and is willing to give you the benefit of that experience. Mentors can be parents, coaches, teachers, boosters, or other athletes. Whether you are still in college, starting a career, or working on an advanced degree, you need a mentor or two. Young people often avoid the company of older people and just hang out together. Sometimes they talk as if they knew everything and older people know nothing. What a way to rob yourself of the valuable experience older friends can provide! Seek out mentors. They can help keep you focused and motivated when you're going through the rough spots. Many busy and successful people are willing to share what they know. It's not charity nor a one-way street. Successful people recognize the value of all the support and guidance they received along the way. They develop a need to give back to the community. And successful people benefit in many ways by surrounding themselves with up-and-coming young people, including staying in touch with new and emerging developments. Hopefully you'll look back on the people who helped you and want to become a mentor yourself.

Getting into graduate school

Whether you are planning on going to medical school, law school, or getting a Master's Degree or Ph.D in science or liberal arts, the program is likely to have admissions requirements beyond simply a college degree. There will be particular majors you must have, and even particular courses. Getting into the graduate program of your choice can be extremely competitive, like trying to break into pro sports. Special projects and extracurricular activities may enhance your credentials. Determine the requirements as early in your undergraduate career as possible.

A mentor can be critical to your success. Often a professor in your department can provide tremendous help and encouragement in keeping you on track. Even as an undergraduate, consider joining the academic association in your field and going to its regional conferences and annual national meetings. These groups usually have special low membership rates for students. By participating in the activities of your academic association, you may find yourself working and socializing with professors who will be evaluating your graduate school applications. Such contact can only increase your chances of admission. You may also be able to get published as an undergraduate, even if only in the form of participating in writing an article that appears on the Web site of an association. This too will help your cause.

Good luck!

If you concentrated on getting an education, not just a degree, and you took full advantage of your athletic experience, you will likely find yourself in the enviable position of having many options. You may be starting a challenging job or graduate school program. Or you may even have the opportunity to continue your sport beyond college. Even if you're one of that select few, the skills you developed in college will prepare you for success in the business of professional sports.

Every athlete knows how important luck can be. A bounce can decide a game, an opponent's flu can decide a meet. Yet we did not include luck among the ingredients for success in Chapter 3. That's because we know that if you stayed off those short cuts that turn into blind alleys, you've prepared yourself to make the most of the breaks that will come your way. So, now we wish you good luck, confident that you have the tools for success.

POSTGAME

by Mike Krzyzewski

Top college basketball programs are the focus of intense media analysis and commentary during the preseason. This hype puts unfair pressures on young people. College teams change too much for anyone to predict in September what the outcome will be in March. I tell my players that my only expectation is that they get better each game. Success means working hard, improving individual skills and teamwork, being part of something that's fun. It means developing trust and friendship, and having an experience that will remain with our athletes for the rest of their lives. Success also means embracing education and graduating prepared for a career. We're proud of our Conference and National Championships, and of our players who have gone on to the NBA. All of our hard work and teamwork led to those results. But there are over 300 Division I basketball teams, and each season only one wins the National Championship. Does that mean there are 300 failures? No—teams that work hard and grow together as teammates and people are successful.

Reach your potential

It takes maturity to focus on working together for constant improvement, rather than dwelling on the most recent victory or defeat. The greatest thing an athlete, or any student, can accomplish in college is to become more mature, to develop the long-term outlook necessary for success. Maturity enabled our 1991 team to defeat UNLV on the way to the national championship, after having lost to them by 30 points the year before. Maturity turns a good team into a great team.

What is maturity? The dictionary defines maturity as "reaching full growth and development." That definition works for fresh fruit, but I believe successful people never stop growing. I learn something about coaching from every practice and every game. At Duke, we try to recruit young men who are already mature enough to understand that they don't know all the answers. (That's important, as I don't even know all the questions.) These men are coachable because they want to improve. They listen, and think about what they hear. They learn from mistakes.

Another part of maturity is taking responsibility not only for yourself, but for your team, and helping lead the team, on the court and off. As a coach, I am a teacher, dedicated to helping my players be the best they can be, in athletics and life in general. I am not, and I don't want to be, a policeman. We all make mistakes; I don't expect anyone to be perfect. But maturity is about understanding how your actions affect you and your teammates, who depend upon you. Mature players tend to base their decisions on long-term goals rather than momentary gratification.

Numbers don't tell us who we are

Selecting a college challenges a high school senior to become more mature. It's too easy to pick a college for an emotional reason: your friend went there, someone says you're great, the team gets lots of TV exposure. Or because of pressure from a parent, friend, or coach. *The Guide* shows you how to select the college that will best prepare you for the rest of your life. It works—if you and your family put in the time to gather the information, weigh all the factors, and make a careful decision. When you're talking to the coach or making a campus visit, don't expect—and don't settle for—a magic carpet ride. Get a realistic portrait of the program, of life as a student there, and, most important, of the educational opportunities. When recruiting is based in reality—not hype—you and your future coach set the tone for an honest, open, trusting relationship that will benefit both of you for four years and beyond.

What sort of person are you? Think a minute before you answer. The answer has nothing to do with scoring 30 points a game, rushing for 1,000 yards in a season, or hitting 50 home runs. Those are numbers; they don't tell us who we are. To perform well as an athlete, though, you need to develop qualities such as poise, teamwork, determination, integrity, selflessness. These are the same qualities that lead to success in any area.

Sports can be a funny thing. Sometimes chance, injuries, the way the ball bounces seems to determine the difference between winning and losing. In the long run, though, hard work and preparation pay off. Life is the same way. What do you do when you want success now, but things don't go your way? That's the great test. Do you give up, or dig down even deeper, knowing your efforts will be rewarded? Sports can be your gateway to an education, a set of values, perhaps even a profession. Whatever your choices in life, remember that success is measured not by numbers but by maturity and character.

Good luck with selecting a college, and with having fun and getting a fine education once you are there.

Mike Krzyzewski (Coach K) is head basketball coach at Duke University. His Blue Devils won NCAA Championships in 1991 and 1992.

APPENDIX A

MESSAGE TO PARENTS

As a parent of a young child, you have more influence than anyone else over how that child develops. As your child grows older, he or she assumes more responsibility, but you still play an important supporting role.

You can give enormous leadership, help, comfort, and inspiration to your child. Or, you can add to the kid's problems. We've all seen parents who make mistakes. Let's face it, sometimes we are those other parents. We love our kids, so we are ready to learn from our mistakes, just as we want to help our kids learn from theirs.

Having fun is number one

Kids naturally play to have fun, and sports are organized ways to play. Kids can learn teamwork, discipline, concentration, goal setting, and sportsmanship from athletics. But only if they are enjoying it. The minute sports become a drag, a chore, or a source of anxiety, the experience changes into something that will hinder rather than help a child's development.

You can have a decisive role in whether sports are fun for your kids. Be there for them, especially when they are disappointed after a defeat (or what they perceive as a defeat). Tell your kids how well they played, how far they've progressed, how proud you are of the work they have put in, and of their sportsmanship. If you are involved in teaching your child athletic

skills, be sure that you are doing far more encouraging than correcting. Kids do not want to constantly hear a list of their failings. (Neither do adults, for that matter.) Remember that progress takes time and effort. Sometimes our children are not the only ones who want instant gratification.

Don't be a "Little League parent"

Don't be the proverbial "Little League parent." Those are parents who scream at their kids for making mistakes, and who scream at umpires and managers. These parents think that a 10-and-Under League game between the True Value Cubs and the A&W Braves is the seventh game of the World Series. Little League parents can be found in any sport. They stress performance over participation. They think winning is everything, and they live through their children's success or failure.

If another dad or mom is acting like a Little League parent, tactfully point out how harmful this behavior is to that parent's child and to all the other kids.

Select the right coach

One of the best contributions you can make as a parent is to save your son or daughter from playing under a "Little League coach"—a coach in any sport at any level who carries on like a Little League parent. All good coaches believe in hard work, appropriate to an athlete's age and skill. But some coaches motivate their kids by cursing at them, insulting them, and generally disrespecting them. Young athletes can be attracted to harsh, tyrannical coaches who have winning records. But no number of wins is worth the psychological damage that these negative types inflict on kids.

If your kid wants to play for a college coach of this sort, and understands what he or she is getting into, and is tough enough to handle it, that's one thing. But no kid should have to play for one of these monsters in high school or earlier, nor do kids at that age have the experience to make an informed decision to do so. The greatest coaches are people like John Wooden, patient teachers who love their athletes. They produce two kinds of victories: they win games and, more importantly, they mold athletes into mature, responsible adults.

Don't be the coach if you're not

You know your kid better than anybody, so it's always tempting to advise the coach that your son or daughter should be playing more, or playing in a different position, or is better than someone else's kid.

Imagine how you'd feel as a coach if every parent bombarded you with such suggestions. Once you feel that you've found a decent coach, be supportive, sit back, and enjoy the game. If you know enough about the sport to help your kid learn a particular skill, away from practice, that's fine. But don't set yourself up as the coach's competitor.

Listen to your kids

To help your kids, you need to know what is on their minds, what they are struggling over internally. Find out by listening more than talking, by asking more than telling.

Sometimes our kids tell us what they think we want to hear. It takes patience and understanding to get to the bottom of things. We can't do it if we are busy imposing our identities on our children rather than helping them develop their own. Parents should be courageous enough to ask their children why they are playing their sport. If the answer is not "to have fun" or if there is little enthusiasm, something is wrong. A good thing might have turned into a bad thing. Take two friends that love basketball. They go out every day to shoot baskets and play in pick up games. They play until it's so dark they can't see the rim. They get into an organized high school program. They both look great on the court. But while one thrives on the pressure, the other hates it and finds that the sport has become a miserable experience. The kid who hates it may be afraid to say so, particularly if the parent projects the attitude that success equals being a star athlete, and that not competing means being a "quitter." It can be a real struggle for a parent to understand that the child may not feel the same way.

A similar problem—and opportunity—arises when your son or daughter is faced with selecting a college. You may have strong feelings about where your kid should go. Maybe you went there, or you love the coach, or it's nearby, or it's got a great pre-med program. But to be helpful, you need to be open to hearing what your son or daughter wants to get out of college. You don't have to agree with your kid. But if you don't seek out his or her views, your opinions will probably receive the same lack of attention. Ideally, you and your kid will be open with each other, and you'll both come out of the discussion with more than you came in with. College selection/recruitment puts pressure on your family. Your ties with your son or daughter can get weaker or stronger. As the experienced adult in the situation, it's primarily up to you. (For a detailed discussion of the issues involved in college selection/recruitment, see Chapters 8, 9, and 10.)

Your help will be appreciated...

Kids need to be able to count on love and support from their parents, no matter the circumstances. A parent best expresses that love and support by being open, by truly listening, and then, if the kid is open to advice at that time, by offering sound reasoning about what to do. If the kid doesn't immediately accept that reasoning, give him or her time to think about it. While it's good to be clear and firm about your convictions, nagging rarely helps.

Your son or daughter may dream of becoming a professional athlete. Maybe you share that dream. Working hard to achieve that goal can be productive and rewarding—unless it leads to ignoring academic and social progress. In this book we emphasize that out of the millions of youngsters engaged in sports, only a small percentage will become professional athletes. Every athlete, no matter how talented, is an injury away from the end of his or her athletic career. Concentrating solely on athletics is a foolish gamble that puts too much pressure on a kid and his family. Sooner or later, it takes the fun out of competing. As a parent, anything you can do to help your kid grasp this truth will be appreciated...eventually.

Appendix B

Questions to Ask Yourself

As we said in the beginning of *The Guide*, we've got to keep in touch with our values to make sure that our actions serve our long range interests. To do that, ask yourself the following questions, along with any others you think are important for you. It would be great if you wrote down your answers, so you could refer to them from time to time. But even thinking about these questions will help you set your priorities. When you need to make an important decision, look at your answers. See if you still feel the same way. Then make a decision that fits your answers.

Successful people, such as Michael Jordan or Bill Gates, founder of the Microsoft Corporation, have written their goals on paper, reviewed them, and kept track of their progress. Written goals are a constant reminder of where you want to go. They help you avoid distractions and stay focused. (If you are still motivated mainly by money, not the journey, we should mention that Bill Gates is the richest man in America. MJ isn't short of lunch money either.)

These questions have no single correct answers, and you may have multiple answers to many of them.

Questions about athletics

- What am I trying to achieve? A career as a professional athlete? An Olympic medal? A successful and enjoyable time at college pursuing my sport? To become as good as I can?

- Why do I want this? Competition? Fun? Fitness? Fame? Money? Self satisfaction?

- Do I like being an athlete and participating in my sport? What do I like about it? What do I dislike about it?

- What would I do if an injury today prevented me from competing in my sport ever again?

- Am I learning values, habits, and skills from my sport that are transferable to other activities? What are they? Sportsmanship? Discipline? Working hard? Teamwork? Ability to think? How can I apply what I'm learning to academic work? To relationships with family, friends, associates?

- Am I learning values, habits, and skills from academics and other areas outside athletics that I could apply to my sport? What are they?

Questions about academics and career

- Which subjects do I like? Why? Which do I hate? Why? Could I do well in these subjects anyway? How?

- What do I want to know about beyond sports? Why? Because it's better to know than not to know? To make a living? For the enjoyment of developing my mind?

- How do I want to earn a living? Have I considered alternatives? If I plan to be a professional athlete, how do I want to earn my living if that doesn't work out? If I don't know yet (perfectly natural in a young person), is it important to me to have a plan to find out? What's the next step in making a plan?

Questions about me and society

- What are my values? Where do they come from? Philosophy? Religion? Family? Friends?

- Are family ties important to me? What kinds of relationships do I want to build with my parents (or those who have been parents to me)? With (eventually) a spouse? With children?

- Is it important to tell the truth? How do I feel about lying? What about cheating at school?

- Should I drink alcohol? Use drugs?

- What principles should govern my behavior with girlfriends or boyfriends? Am I ready to engage in sexual relationships?

- What do I believe now about social and political questions? How might my views change as I become older? Is it important to me to play a role in deciding social issues? To be involved in the issues affecting my community?

- What's good about my friends? What isn't? What kind of friends do I want?

- What's good about me? What isn't? What do I want to change? How can I do it? Who can help me?

- Do I consider myself a member of a community? What community? My team? My school? My neighborhood? My country? My ethnic group? The global community? Can I belong to more than one community?

- What do I want to get out of life?

The final group of questions, about you and society, is the most basic. If your answers to the sports and academics questions are not in line with your answers to the social questions, you've got some rethinking to do.

Your answers, taken together, set out your goals. Select a college that will help you achieve those goals. Focus on actions that bring you closer to those goals.

APPENDIX C

IMPORTANT CONTACT INFO

Athlete Network
PO Box 34867
Los Angeles, CA 90034
www.athletenetwork.com

The Real Athletes Guide: How to succeed in sports, school, and life

The Real Athletes Pro Guide (coming in 1999)

National Collegiate Athletic Association (NCAA)
6201 College Blvd.
Overland Park, KS 66211-2422
(913) 339-1906
NCAA Hotline (800) 638-3731
www.ncaa.org

NCAA Guide for the College-Bound Student-Athlete

Making Sure You Are Eligible to Participate in College Sports

NCAA Transfer Guide

A Career in Professional Athletics:
A Guide For Making the Transition

NCAA Initial-Eligibility Clearinghouse
PO Box 4044
Iowa City, IA 52243-4044
(319) 337-1492
24-Hour Voice Response Service
(319) 339-3003

National Association of Intercollegiate Athletics (NAIA)
6120 S. Yale Ave.
Suite 1450
Tulsa, OK 74136
(918) 494-8828
www.naia.org

A Guide for the College-Bound Student

Guide for Students Transferring from Two-Year Institutions

National Junior College Athletic Association (NJCAA)
PO 7305
Colorado Springs, CO 80933-7305
(719) 590-9788
www.njcaa.org

Information for a Prospective NJCAA Student-Athlete

National Small College Athletic Association (NSCAA)
113 East Bow Street
Franklin, NH 03235
users.lr.net/~dmagee/

National Christian College Athletic Association (NCCAA)
PO Box 1312
Marion, IN 46952
(765) 674-8401
www.bright.net/~nccaa

College Board (SAT)
PO Box 6200
Princeton, NJ 08541-6200
(609) 771-7600
www.collegeboard.org

ACT
PO Box 414
Iowa City, IA 52243-0414
(319) 337-1270
www.act.org

Collegiate Directories
PO Box 450640
Cleveland, OH 44145
(800) 426-2232
www.collegiatedirectories.com

The National Directory of College Athletics

APPENDIX D

USEFUL WEB SITES

Preparing for college

Athlete Network	AthleteNetwork.com
College Edge	collegeedge.com
Collegiate Directories	collegiatedirectories.com
US News	usnews.com/usnews/edu
Yahoo!	yahoo.com/education

SAT and ACT

College Board	collegeboard.org
ACT Assessment	act.org
Princeton Review	review.com/college
Peterson's	petersons.com

Athletic Associations

NAIA	naia.org
NCAA	ncaa.org
NCCAA	bright.net/~nccaa
NJCAA	njcaa.org
NSCAA	users.lr.net/~dmagee

Jobs and career

Job Trak	jobtrak.com
Student Center	studentcenter.com

General Interest

Amateur Athletic Foundation	aafla.org
Amazon.com	amazon.com
CNN and Sports Illustrated	cnnsi.com
ESPN	espn.com
Life's Playbook	lifesplaybook.com
Women's Sports Foundation	lifetimetv.com/wosport

Index

ORDER FORM

To Order, Call Toll Free: 800/356-9315

Item	Quantity	Price	Total
The Real Athletes Guide		$19.95	

CA residents add 8.25% sales tax		
$4 shipping for first book, $1 for each additional copy		
Total		

Mail:
Athlete Network
PO Box 34867
Los Angeles, CA 90034

Please make check payable to **Athlete Network Press.**

Name _____

Address _____

City/State/Zip _____

Phone or email _____

Address to send to (if different from above)

Name _____

Address _____

City/State/Zip _____

Fax Your Order:

Fax: 800/242-0036

❑ Visa   ❑ MasterCard   ❑ AmEx   ❑ Discover

Account # _____ Exp. _____

ORDER FORM

To Order, Call Toll Free: 800/356-9315

Item	Quantity	Price	Total
The Real Athletes Guide		$19.95	

CA residents add 8.25% sales tax

$4 shipping for first book,
$1 for each additional copy

Mail: **Total**
Athlete Network
PO Box 34867
Los Angeles, CA 90034

Please make check payable to **Athlete Network Press.**

Name   _____

Address   _____

City/State/Zip _____

Phone or email _____

Address to send to (if different from above)

Name   _____

Address   _____

City/State/Zip _____

Fax Your Order:

Fax: 800/242-0036

❏ Visa   ❏ MasterCard   ❏ AmEx   ❏ Discover

Account # _____ Exp. _____